Did you ever have the experience in s... blackboard? When the slate has bee... nothing at all had ever been written on it. This is what God does for us when we come to Him, confessing our sin and trusting Christ as our Savior and Lord…. The slate is wiped clean! Only God can do that. We can't do it ourselves…. Resolve right now to allow God to wipe your slate clean by confessing your sins and letting Him give you a brand new start.

If we confess our sins, He is faithful and just
to forgive us our sins, and to cleanse us from
all unrighteousness. 1 JOHN 1:9

JULY 1

I have found in my travels that those who keep heaven in view remain serene and cheerful in the darkest day. If the glories of heaven were more real to us, if we lived less for material things and more for things eternal and spiritual, we would be less easily disturbed by this present life…. In these days of darkness and upheaval and uncertainty, the trusting and forward-looking Christian remains optimistic and joyful, knowing that Christ someday must rule, and "if we endure, we shall also reign with Him" (2 Timothy 2:12).

JUNE 30

God doesn't want us to isolate ourselves. In praying for His disciples Jesus said, "As You sent Me into the world, I also have sent them into the world" (John 17:18). If we isolate ourselves from others, we have no impact and demonstrate a lack of love. But neither does God want us to become like the unbelieving world.... The Bible warns, "All that is in the world—the lust of the flesh, the lust of the eyes, and the pride of life—is not of the Father but is of the world" (1 John 2:16). Let Christ fill your life, and there won't be any room for the world.

JULY 2

Imagine in your mind a ferocious ocean storm beating against the rocky shore. The lightning flashes, the thunder roars, the waves lash the rocks. But then imagine that you see a crevice in the rocky cliff—and inside is a little bird, its head serenely tucked under its wing, fast asleep.... God promised Moses, "I will put you in the cleft of the rock, and will cover you with My hand" (Exodus 33:22). That is God's promise to us. Christ is our Rock, and we are secure in His hands forever. The storm rages, but our hearts are at rest.

JUNE 29

Sin cost God His very best. Is it any wonder the angels veiled their faces and were silent in their consternation as they witnessed the outworking of God's plan? How inconceivable it must have seemed to them, when they considered the fearful depravity of sin, that Jesus should shoulder it all. But they were soon to unveil their faces and offer their praises again. A light was kindled that day at Calvary—"the light of the gospel of the glory of Christ, who is the image of God" (2 Corinthians 4:4).... Has the light of the gospel shone in your heart? And is it shining through you to others?

JULY 3

When we come to Christ, the Bible says He imparts His righteousness to us. Once we were sinners in God's eyes; now He sees us as righteous because of Christ. Did we deserve it? No. Did we earn it? No. It is all grace—all because of God's favor by our deeds, no matter how good we are. Only Christ can save us. Thank God that you now stand before Him, clothed in the perfect righteousness of Christ.

He made Him...to be sin for us, that we might become the righteousness of God in Him.

2 CORINTHIANS 5:21

JUNE 28

During the national observance of the one-hundredth anniversary of the Statue of Liberty in New York Harbor, I was struck by the great emphasis on the number of immigrants who had often left everything behind. Coming to America with nothing but the clothes on their backs, they risked their lives for something they valued more highly than everything they had left behind: freedom…. Their experience is a picture of what we must do when we come to Christ. We must forsake our allegiance to this world, leave behind all that it offers, and become citizens of a new kingdom—the Kingdom of God. His statue of liberty is in the form of the Cross.

JULY 4

Some years ago someone gave my little boy a dollar. He brought it to me and said, "Daddy, keep this for me." But in a few minutes he came back and said, "Daddy, I'd better keep my own dollar." He tucked it in his pocket and went out to play. In a few minutes he came back with tears in his eyes, saying, "Daddy, I lost my dollar. Help me find it." How often we commit our burdens to the Lord and then fail to trust Him by taking matters into our own hands…. The Bible's promise is true: "Blessed is the man who makes the Lord His trust" (Psalm 40:4 NIV).

JUNE 27

We do not understand the intricate patterns of the stars in their courses, but we know that He who created them does, and that just as surely as He guides them, He is charting a safe course for us. The next time you look into the heavens at night, remember the words of the Psalmist: "The heavens declare the glory of God" (Psalm 19:1).

Oh, the depth of the riches both of the wisdom and knowledge of God! ROMANS 11:33

JULY 5

Some time ago a university professor was quoted as saying, "There are two things that will never be solved—the problems of race and war." Perhaps he was right; only time will tell. Admittedly, however, the Bible gives us little reason for optimism about any lasting solution to these problems. Both racism and war have their origin in the pride and covetousness of the human heart.... The Bible calls Christ the "Prince of Peace" (Isaiah 9:6). He shattered the prejudices of His day by reaching out to those of another race, and He expects no less of us.... Ask God to help you be an instrument of His love to those around you.

JUNE 26

If the angels rejoice over one sinner who repents (Luke 15:10), then the angelic hosts are numbered among the spectators in the heavenly grandstands. They are included among those who are referred to as "so great a cloud of witnesses" (Hebrews 12:1); and they never miss any of the details of our earthly pilgrimage. Nor does our God—Father, Son, and Holy Spirit—overlook what goes on here. As the Bible says, "All things are...open to the eyes of Him to whom we must give account" (Hebrews 4:13).

Since we are surrounded by so great a cloud of witnesses, let us lay aside every weight.
HEBREWS 12:1

JULY 6

King Rehoboam stubbornly rejected the wise advice of his nation's elders and instead followed those who told him only what he wanted to hear. As a result, conflict broke out and the nation divided. The Bible warns, "Whatever a man sows, that he will also reap" (Galatians 6:7). Life is filled with decisions—some minor, but some life changing. How will you make them? The most important thing I can tell you is this: Seek God's will in every decision. Pray. Turn to the Scriptures. Seek the advice of godly friends. Ask the Holy Spirit to guide you. God loves you, and His way is always best.

JUNE 25

I once read about a sundial on which was inscribed the cryptic message, "It is later than you think." Travelers would often pause to meditate on the meaning of that phrase....

We Christians have a sundial—the Word of God. From Genesis to Revelation it bears its warning: "It is later than you think." Writing to the Christians of his day Paul said, "It is already the hour for you to awaken from sleep; for now salvation is nearer to us than when we believed.... Learn to live each day as if it were your last. Some day it will be.

JULY 7

You can scrub a pig, sprinkle Chanel No. 5 on him, put a ribbon around his neck, and take him into your living room. But when you turn him loose, he will jump into the first mud puddle he sees because his nature has never been changed. He is still a pig.... The Bible teaches that when we come to Christ, we are spiritually born again. God's Spirit comes to live within us and change us. Our motives change, our objectives change, our dispositions change, our eternal destiny changes.... It begins now, as we open our hearts to Him. Is your life "being transformed...from glory to glory"?

JUNE 24

God is a spirit. He does not have a body, nor is He confined to one place (as a physical being would be). At the same time, He has the attributes of a person: He thinks, He speaks, He communicates, He loves, He becomes angry, He grieves. Because God is a person, He feels what we feel. No matter what we face, He understands what we are going through. He even understands our temptations, for Christ "has been tempted in every way, just as we are—yet...without sin" (Hebrews 4:15 NIV). And that is why you can bring anything—anything—to Him in prayer, confident that He will understand.

JULY 8

When the apostle Paul asked God to remove his "thorn in the flesh," God did not remove it, saying instead, "My grace is sufficient for you" (2 Corinthians 12:9). Rather than complain or become angry at God, Paul joyfully submitted to God's will. He discovered that God's grace truly was sufficient, even in the midst of pain. Christ desires to be with you in whatever crisis you may find yourself. Call upon His name. See if He will not do as He promised He would. He may not make your problems go away, but He will give you the power to deal with them and to overcome them by His grace.

JUNE 23

God is the only source of true happiness, because He offers those intangibles that we mistakenly believe can be found on earth: contentment, security, peace, and hope for the future. None of these can be found in a job, a human relationship, money, power, or position. They are God's alone to give…. The Lord Jesus, in His Sermon on the Mount, told where ultimate happiness lies: "Blessed are those who hunger and thirst for righteousness, for they shall be filled" (Matthew 5:6). This is God's promise—and it is true. Riches…or righteousness? Which will be your goal?

JULY 9

Although the doctrine of the Trinity is difficult for us to understand, the Bible teaches that He is co-equal with God the Father and co-equal with God the Son. The Bible also teaches that the Holy Spirit is a Person. He is never to be referred to as "it."... He is a mighty Person, the Holy Spirit of God. The Bible tells us as well that He is omnipotent...He has all power. It tells us also that He is omnipresent...He is everywhere at the same time.... With the seventeenth-century Anglican bishop, Jeremy Taylor, I can say, "It is impossible for that man to despair who remembers that his Helper is omnipotent."

JUNE 22

To have peace with God and to have the peace of God in our hearts is not enough. This vertical relationship must have a horizontal outworking, or our faith is in vain. Jesus said that we were to love the Lord with all our hearts and our neighbors as ourselves. This dual love for God and others is like the positive and negative poles of a battery—unless both connections are made, we have no power.... If we have peace with God and the peace of God, we will become peacemakers.... Is the peace of Christ in your life overflowing to others?

JULY 10

During the early years of the twentieth century, Bill Borden turned his back on one of America's great family fortunes to become a missionary to China. He only got as far as Egypt where, still in his twenties, he died of typhoid fever. Before his death he wrote, "No reserves, no retreats, no regrets!" Discipleship is always costly.... It will cost us...our plans, our wills, our selfish desires. Jesus' standard has not changed: "If anyone desires to come after Me, let him deny himself and take up his cross, and follow Me" (Matthew 16:24).... Follow Christ, and at life's end you will be able to say, "No regrets!"

JUNE 21

Many today say there is no such thing as absolute truth. From philosophers to pop musicians, the word goes out that "truth" is only what you want it to be, and what is "true" for you isn't necessarily "true" for anyone else. But Jesus Christ is absolute truth. Dozens of times He declares, "I tell you the truth." In one of His boldest and most uncompromising statements He affirmed, "I am the way, the truth, and the life" (John 14:6).... Do not be misled by the moral and spiritual relativity of our age. God has revealed His truth to us—in His written Word, the Bible, and in the living Word, Jesus Christ.

JULY 11

Several years ago a university student asked me what had been my biggest surprise in life. Immediately I replied, "The brevity of life." Almost before we know it, the years have passed and life is almost over. On one hand, life's brevity should challenge us. If ever we are to live for Christ and share Him with others, it must be now. Jesus said, "The night is coming when no one can work" (John 9:4). But life's brevity should also comfort us. Life is short—and before us is eternity!... Don't live as if this life will continue forever. It won't. Live instead with eternity in view!

JUNE 20

C.S. Lewis once said that we tend to make one of two errors about Satan: We either make too little of him, or we make too much. The same could be said of angels. Don't make too little of them. God has given "His angels charge over you, to keep you in all your ways" (Psalm 91:11). On the other hand, don't worship them or become preoccupied with them. Instead, thank God for His angels and rejoice in their unseen watchfulness over you.

His angels...keep you in all your ways.
PSALM 91:11

JULY 12

We should seek to produce the fruit of the Spirit in our lives. Or to put it more accurately, we should allow the Holy Spirit to produce His fruit in our lives. You say, "I am powerless to produce such fruit. You don't know how weak and self-centered I am. It would be utterly impossible for me to do so!" With that I agree! That is, we can't produce this fruit in our own strength.... Our responsibility is to cultivate the soil of our hearts through sincere devotion and surrender, so He might find favorable ground to produce His fruit.

The fruit of the Spirit is love, joy, peace,...
gentleness, self-control. GALATIANS 5:22-23

JUNE 19

God offers spiritual "training" to build us up inside in much the same way that physical exercise can build us up on the outside. He has also provided all the resources we need to defend ourselves and keep Satan at bay. These include the Bible, prayer, faith, righteous living, and the Holy Spirit within us. But, like physical training, we must be diligent in their application. God has not promised to shield us from trouble, but He has promised to protect us in the midst of trouble. Most of all, never forget that because of Christ's death and resurrection, Satan is already a defeated foe—and some day the war will be over.

JULY 13

At times, we may think of ourselves as morally good and decent; we are content that "we are not like other men." But compared to God's purity, we are defiled and filthy.

In spite of our sins and uncleanness, God still loves us. And because He loves us, He decided to provide for us a purity we could never attain on our own.... Thank God today that you are now "whiter than snow," because "you were washed...in the name of the Lord Jesus and by the Spirit of our God" (1 Corinthians 6:11)!

Wash me, and I shall be whiter than snow.
PSALM 51:7

JUNE 18

Paul looked forward to death with great anticipation. He said, "For to me, to live is Christ, and to die is gain" (Philippians 1:21). Death for him was not an enemy to be feared, but a reality to be welcomed, in God's time. For him death was the joyous gateway to new life—the life of heaven. Without the resurrection of Christ there could be no hope for the future. The Bible promises that someday we are going to stand face to face with the resurrected Christ. All our questions will be answered, and all our sorrows and fears will vanish.

We are looking for a city that is to come.
HEBREWS 13:14 NRSV

JULY 14

Prayer links us with God's true purposes, for us and for the world. It not only brings the blessings of God's will to our own personal lives, it brings us the added blessing of being in step with God's plan. Prayer also—in ways we will never fully understand this side of eternity—makes us partners with God in what He is doing in the world. God works through our prayers!

Whatever you ask in My name, that I will do.
JOHN 14:13

JUNE 17

Our oldest daughter married a Swiss, and they often spend their summers in Switzerland. Sometimes we have visited them there and have gone soaring over the countryside on chair lifts high in the Alps. Looking down we can see almost a carpet of wildflowers, some of the most beautiful in the world. Only a few months before, those plants were buried under heavy snow. Yet that snow prepared the way for their growth—providing them with water, and even insulating them from the winter winds. Our burdens can be like that snow, preparing the way for something beautiful once the winter is past.

JULY 15

Occasionally I see reports of happenings that cannot be humanly explained—of visitors unexpectedly appearing to assist in times of crisis, or warning of impending danger. These can only be explained as the intervention of God's angels. In the Bible, angels occasionally assumed visible form—at the birth of Jesus, for example. But usually angels go about their business unseen and unrecognized. They never draw attention to themselves, but point us instead to Christ.

JUNE 16

A driver stopped to ask the way to a certain street. When told, he asked doubtfully, "Is that the best way?" The man replied, "That is the only way." There is only one way of salvation—and that is Christ…. Is this arrogance or intolerance? No—and Christians must never be guilty of those attitudes. We are saved solely by God's grace; we do not deserve it…. If you have never done so, turn to Christ today. And if you do know Him, pray today for someone you know who does not yet believe, and ask God to help you tell that person of His salvation.

No one comes to the Father except through Me.
JOHN 14:6

JULY 16

Unfortunately, worry is an ingrained habit for most of us. But because we are God's children, He is responsible for our welfare. That is why you should be "casting all your care upon Him, for He cares for you" (1 Peter 5:7).

In other words, let God do the worrying! He says, "I'll take the burden—don't give it a thought—leave it to Me."

Never forget: God is bigger than your problems. Whatever worries press upon you today, put them in God's hands—and leave them there.

As a father pities his children, so the Lord pities those who fear Him. PSALM 103:13

JUNE 15

When I understand something of Christ's love for me as a sinner, I respond with love for Christ—and that love includes feelings and emotions. But emotions come and go, and we must not allow them to mislead us. God loves me, whether I "feel" it or not.... What makes the difference? It can be summarized in one word: commitment.... This commitment not only keeps us faithful to Christ when we don't feel like it; it also keeps away negative emotions such as doubt and fear. John Witherspoon, the only cleric to sign the Declaration of Independence, once said, "It is only the fear of God that can deliver us from the fear of man."

JULY 17

Satan will always try to discourage those who belong to Christ. When problems persist, he may even whisper, "See, God doesn't care about you!" But with the Holy Spirit's help, we can combat the evil one and contradict his lies. If God dismissed all our problems with a single stroke, we would be left defenseless, unequipped to meet the inevitable attacks of the enemy of our souls. But in the midst of life's problems, God supplies everything we need to see us through.

I can do all things through Christ who strengthens me. PHILIPPIANS 4:13

JUNE 14

All through the Bible we see God's patience and perseverance as He pursues misguided and obstinate men and women—men and women who were born to a high destiny as His sons and daughters, but who strayed from His side. From Genesis to Revelation God is constantly saying, "Return to me, and I will return to you." No matter how far you have strayed, God still loves you, and He wants to welcome you home—forever.

JULY 18

The late C.S. Lewis in his remarkable book *Christian Behavior*, said, "Hope is one of the theological virtues." He meant that a continual looking forward to the eternal world is not, as some people think, a form of escapism or wishful thinking, but one of the things a Christian is meant to do.... "Aim at heaven," said Lewis, "and you will get earth thrown in. Aim at earth, and you will get neither."

If I go and prepare a place for you, I will come again. JOHN 14:3

JUNE 13

As we survey the world scene with Bible in hand, we know we do not worship an absentee God. He is standing in the shadows of history, still working to bring His plans to completion.... Every headline, every news report confirms what the prophet Jeremiah said centuries ago: "The heart is deceitful above all things, and desperately wicked; who can know it?" (Jeremiah 17:9). But never forget: God will speak history's final word.... No matter how foreboding the future, the Christian knows the end of the story—and it is glorious! Don't lose heart. The best is yet to be!

Forever, O Lord, Your word is settled in heaven. PSALM 119:89

JULY 19

James did not say, "Count it all joy when you fall into an easy chair." He said, "Count it all joy when you fall into various trials" (James 1:2). Joy is not the same as happiness—although they may overlap. Happiness depends on circumstances; joy depends on God. Happiness vanishes when life turns painful; joy keeps going and may even grow. Joy comes from a living, vital relationship with God. It comes from knowing this world is only temporary, and some day we will be with God forever.... It comes from a life of submission to the Holy Spirit—regardless of circumstances.

JUNE 12

Often, I hear someone introduced this way: "This is Bob and he works for...," as if where a person works or what a person does determines his or her value. (I have noticed it is usually only the well-to-do or those who are thought of as "successful" who are introduced this way.) Yet God does not judge us by our success.... Our value comes from the fact that God made us and loves us, and Christ died for us. Our value comes from the fact that He adopted us into His family, and we are now His children forever.... Get your identity from Christ, for you are infinite worth to Him!

JULY 20

You and I have the incredible privilege of approaching the God of the Universe.... We can only do this because Jesus Christ has opened the way.

We are to pray in times of adversity, lest we become faithless and unbelieving.

We are to pray in times of prosperity, lest we become boastful and proud.

We are to pray in times of danger, lest we become fearful and doubting.

We are to pray in times of security, lest we become self-sufficient.

Pray believing, in the promise of God's Word that
"If we ask anything according to His will,
He hears us" (1 John 5:14).

JUNE 11

Haydn, the great musician, was once asked why his church music was so cheerful. He replied, "When I think upon God, my heart is so full of joy that the notes dance and leap, as it were, from my pen, and since God has given me a cheerful heart, it will be pardoned me that I serve Him with a cheerful spirit." Haydn had discovered the secret to lasting joy: "I think on God." Looking at our circumstances won't bring us to lasting joy. It may even make us depressed or angry. But when we "think on God"—when we turn our minds and hearts to His power and His love for us, we can't help but be joyful.

JULY 21

When we purchase something of great value—a house, for example—we are usually required to put down a deposit to indicate our sincerity and to promise that our intentions are serious…. God has made some incredible promises to us—promises that stagger our imaginations. He has promised that we might have a relationship with Him through His Son. He has promised never to leave us or forsake us and to be with us always. He has promised to take us to heaven when we die…. Not only is Jesus Christ a sufficient "down payment" on God's promises, He is, in fact, payment in full!

JUNE 10

At the moment we see only our immediate problems and burdens, but God sees the whole. He sees not only the present, but the future as well. He wants to lift us above ourselves. He wants us to see everything in light of His plans. The Psalmist said, "The Lord will perfect that which concerns me" (Psalm 138:8). Don't get bogged down. Keep your eyes on God, for He sees the whole picture, and He knows what is best for you. You can trust Him, because He loves you.

JULY 22

Some things in life cannot be changed—and some can. Some things God has given to us as fixed realities that we must accept. And some things He would have us not accept, but (with His help) work to change. If we fail to do both of these—to accept some things and work to change others—we will end up burdened with worry, undeserved guilt, and frustration. Someone once said, "Worry is the interest paid on trouble before it comes due." Instead, God would have us learn to trust Him. "Cast your burden on the Lord, and He shall sustain you" (Psalm 55:22).

JUNE 9

In big cities I often see wrecking balls destroying our old structures to make way for new ones. Some of the "old structures" in America are less than a hundred years old. In Europe, buildings several centuries old are common. But even those buildings will eventually be destroyed, by a natural disaster if not by man. Only what is built on the solid foundation of Christ will last. Jesus said, "Everyone who hears these words of mine and puts them into practice is like a wise man who built his house on the rock" (Matthew 7:24 NIV). Are you listening to God's Word and putting it into practice every day?

JULY 23

God has given our conscience to us. Its very presence is a reflection of God in the human soul. Sin, however, can dull or even distort our conscience, silencing its voice and leading us astray. But God's Word can purify and sharpen our conscience—and when that happens, "He leads [us] in paths of righteousness for His name's sake" (Psalm 23:3). Is this happening in your life?

I myself always strive to have a conscience without offense toward God and men.

Acts 24:16

JUNE 8

Jesus was a gentle and compassionate person. When He came into the world, there were few hospitals, few places of refuge for the poor, few homes for orphans. There were no hospitals to treat the mentally ill, no shelters for the homeless.... Christ changed all that. He healed the sick, fed the hungry, and opened the eyes of the blind.... Wherever true Christianity has gone, His followers have performed acts of kindness, love, and gentleness. Do others see Christ's gentleness and compassion in you?

In everything, do to others what you would have them do to you. MATTHEW 7:12 NIV

JULY 24

God places a seal on us when we receive Christ. And that seal is a person—the Holy Spirit.... The Spirit is also God's pledge. He not only seals the arrangement, but He represents God's commitment to see us through.... Finally, the Spirit witnesses to us, by the Scriptures and within our hearts.... What a wonderful thing to know the Holy Spirit has been given to us as a seal—a pledge—and a witness! May each of these give us new assurance of God's unchanging love for us, and give us confidence as we seek to live for Him.

JUNE 7

Jesus said, "In the world you will have tribulation." He didn't say that you could have tribulation or that if you aren't a good person, tribulation will come your way. Jesus flatly stated you will have tribulation. It is as certain as growing older. But the wonderful promise of Christ is that while you will have trials and tribulations, "Be of good cheer. I have overcome the world" (John 16:33).

JULY 25

We can jump over some barriers in life by our own will and our own efforts; God has not left us completely powerless. But some walls are so high we need more than this.... When we try to jump over them by ourselves, we repeatedly fall short. But with God's help, we can conquer them. What walls do you need to conquer? A habit you cannot break? An emotion that defeats you? An attitude that separates you from others? A heart beset with doubt or discouragement or fear? Whatever it is, with God's help you can leap over a wall.

By my God I can leap over a wall.
PSALM 18:29

JUNE 6

Some people have a warped idea of living the Christian life. Seeing talented, successful Christians, they attempt to imitate them.... But when they discover that their own gifts are different or their contributions are more modest (or even invisible), they collapse in discouragement and overlook genuine opportunities that are open to them.... The key is to realize you are here to serve Christ, not yourself.... He does not call His children to a playground, but to a battleground. In the midst of it all, when we serve Christ, we truly discover that "The joy of the Lord is [our] strength" (Nehemiah 8:10).

JULY 26

Sometimes God removes our trials, and it isn't necessarily wrong to ask Him to do that. But often the trials remain, and when they do, we should accept them and ask God to teach us from them.... It is through the suffering, the tests and trials of life, that we can draw near to God. A. B. Simpson once heard a man say something he never forgot: "When God tests you, it is a good time for you to test Him by putting His promises to the proof, and claiming from Him just as much as your trials have rendered necessary."

JUNE 5

We need to rely constantly on the Holy Spirit. We need to remember that Christ dwells in us through the Holy Spirit.... It is important that we stand aside and let Him take over in all our choices and decisions. We know that the Holy Spirit prays for us (Romans 8:26), and what a comfort that should be to the weakest of us. A victorious Christian is one who, in spite of worries, inner conflicts, and tensions, is confident that God is in control and will be victorious in the end. Whatever our difficulties, whatever our circumstances, we must remember, as Corrie ten Boom used to say, "Jesus is victor!"

JULY 27

We forget that Jesus was human as well as divine.... If the chisel slipped and cut His finger, His blood was red and warm like ours. He knew what it meant to work long hours, to come in at night tired and weary. That is one of the reasons Jesus could say with such appeal, "Come to Me, all you who labor and are heavy laden, and I will give you rest" (Matthew 11:28).... But the greatest work Jesus did was...what He accomplished through the Cross and Resurrection.... And that is why we can come by faith to Him, and He will give us rest.

JUNE 4

When we face decisions, we need to remember that God hasn't left us in the dark, nor is He uninterested. God loves us, and He wants what is best for us. He has a perfect path in life for us, and He wants us to choose it instead of the wrong paths Satan would tempt us to follow.... He also gives us wisdom (sometimes through other people) to understand our situation, and He gives us the Holy Spirit to guide us. Never make a decision without committing it to God and seeking His will. He promises to guide you—and He will.

JULY 28

A great man of God lay on his deathbed. He summoned his grandson to come to his side. Calling the boy's name, he said, "I don't know what type of work I will be doing in heaven, but if it's allowed, I'm going to ask the Lord Jesus to let me help build your mansion. You be sure you send up plenty of the right materials." Living a life of purity and love, leading others to Christ as we share our faith, doing good work in Christ's name—all of these things are materials that may be sent on ahead.... What kind of materials are you sending up to heaven?

JUNE 3

There will always be secrets and motives of God that lie beyond our grasp. God knows everything; we do not. Only in heaven will we understand God's ways more fully. As Paul said, "Now I know in part, but then I shall know just as I also am known" (1 Corinthians 13:12). But based upon what we do know about God's character, demonstrated supremely in the Cross, we can trust that God is doing what is best for us. God says in His Word, "I know the plans I have for you...plans to prosper you and not to harm you, plans to give you hope and a future" (Jeremiah 29:11 NIV).

JULY 29

Someone has said that before our prayers can mean anything to God, they must first mean something to us. Mindlessly repeating a prayer we memorized in childhood, or vaguely asking God to bless everyone, everywhere—that isn't authentic prayer. Prayer is speaking to God about the deepest concerns of our hearts.... God delights in the prayers of His children—prayers that express our love for Him, prayers that share our deepest burdens with Him. Don't pray casually or thoughtlessly, but "come boldly to the throne of grace, that [you] may obtain mercy and find grace to help in time of need" (Hebrews 4:16).

JUNE 2

We get so used to this world that we lose sight of the next. We get so used to the darkness and chaos of this world's suffering and violence that we lose sight of the brightness of Him who alone could say, "I am the light of the world. He who follows Me shall not walk in darkness, but have the light of life" (John 8:12).... Today world leaders struggle with almost insurmountable problems—and they always will. But in the midst of the world's persistent darkness, never lose sight of Jesus. He alone is the hope of the world—and He is your hope as well.

JULY 30

What is troubling you today? Is your heart burdened because of some problem that threatens to overcome you? Are you filled with anxiety and worry, wondering what will happen next? Listen—as a child of God through faith in Christ, you can turn these over to Christ, knowing that He loves you and is able to help you. Don't carry your burden any longer, but bring it "boldly to the throne of grace"—and leave it there.

JUNE 1

John Knox spent much time in prayer, and the Church in Scotland burst into new life. John Wesley prayed long and often, and the Methodist movement was born.

Martin Luther prayed earnestly, and the Reformation exploded across Europe.

Why was prayer so important to these spiritual giants of the past? Because they knew they were up against almost overwhelming forces of spiritual opposition…. God desires that we Christians be concerned and burdened for a lost world. If we pray this kind of prayer, an era of peace may come to the world and wickedness may be turned back. "The effective, fervent prayer of a righteous man avails much" (James 5:16).

JULY 31

One thousand years from this day you will be more alive than you are at this moment. The Bible teaches that life does not end at the cemetery. There is a future life with God for those who put their trust in His Son, Jesus Christ. There is also a future hell of separation from God where all are going who have refused, rejected, or neglected to receive His Son, Jesus Christ. Make sure of your relationship to Christ, and then ask God to help you live each day for His glory.

As for man, his days are like grass; as a flower of the field, so he flourishes. PSALM 103:15

MAY 31

How many times have you heard someone say, "All I can do is pray"? All I can do is pray?! You might as well say to a starving man, "All I can do is offer you food."... Praying unlocks the doors of heaven and releases the power of God. James 4:2 says, "You do not have because you do not ask."... So often our prayers focus only on ourselves. But God wants to use us, through our prayers, to touch the lives of other people as well. For whom should you be praying this day?

Pray without ceasing. 1 THESSALONIANS 5:17

AUGUST 1

One of the primary reasons for the breakdown in the home is that we have forgotten God's command about marriage.... Jesus said, "A man shall leave his father and mother and be joined to his wife.... Therefore what God has joined together, let not man separate" (Matthew 19:5-6).... Marriage is a symbol of the unity between Christ and His church—a unity that should never be torn.... If divorce has happened to you, God can forgive the past, heal the present, and give hope for the future. But if you are married, treasure your spouse as a gift from God, and yield your marriage to Christ.

MAY 30

God hovers over the entire world, seeking to pluck from sin immortal souls who are in danger of "drowning" in hell. He tosses out a line to all those who are in trouble. Some grab on to God's line and freely receive the gift of His Son, Jesus Christ…. But others ignore the line, or even knock it away, believing they are not really in peril, or that they can make it to safety on their own. Tragically, they are lost not because God has rejected them, but because they have rejected God. Don't make the wrong choice!

I have set before you life and death,…
therefore choose life. DEUTERONOMY 30:19

AUGUST 2

The master craftsman knows that years of work, sacrifice, and suffering as an apprentice precede his being promoted to the master of his trade.... The Bible teaches that sacrifice and discipline are necessary if we are to be faithful servants of Christ. Paul wrote, "I discipline my body and bring it into subjection, lest, when I have preached to others, I myself should become disqualified" (1 Corinthians 9:27). Discipline your time... discipline your eyes...discipline your mind...discipline your body...all for the sake of Christ.

Walk in wisdom...redeeming the time.
COLOSSIANS 4:5

MAY 29

The main reason Jesus died on the Cross was to save us from our sins. But the New Testament also stresses the importance of His suffering as an example for us.

The Greek word for example...refers to something written down by the teacher, so it could be followed and copied exactly by a child learning to write. Christ is our copybook.... How did He bear it? By not giving in to despair or doubt. By looking beyond it and seeing the glory that was to come. By knowing the Father was with Him and would use His suffering for good. The same can be true for us.

AUGUST 3

An old saying declares: "All roads lead to Rome." Perhaps it was true in the ancient world—but today you can get lost anywhere!…The only sure way to reach your destination is to consult a good road map or ask someone who knows the way…. Jesus did not say, "I am one of many roads to God." What He said was, "I am the way." That wasn't arrogance, or narrow-mindedness, or lack of compassion. It was truth—because only Christ came from heaven to pay the price for our sins. Follow Christ and never be lost!

I am the way, the truth, and the life. No one comes to the Father except through Me.

JOHN 14:6

MAY 28

Patience is not simply "teeth-clenched" endurance. It is an attitude of expectation. The farmer patiently watches his barren ground because he knows there will be results. He has patience in his labors because there will be products of his labor. So it is in the spiritual realm. God knows the final product of what is happening to us, and He would have us link patience to our faith. Ask God for the gift of patience—and then use it.

The testing of your faith produces patience.
JAMES 1:3

AUGUST 4

There is a story about Martin Luther going through a period of discouragement and depression. For days his long face graced the family table and dampened the family's home life. One day his wife came to the breakfast table all dressed in black…. When Martin asked her who had died, she replied, "Martin, the way you've been behaving lately, I thought God had died, so I came prepared to attend His funeral."… As a result the great Reformer resolved never again to allow worldly care, resentment, depression, discouragement, or frustration to defeat him…. When was the last time you praised God in the midst of despair?… Do it, and then you'll feel like it!

MAY 27

World War I was called "the war to end all wars," but it wasn't. Whether men shoot and fight one another or not, there is "warfare" in the home: warfare between husband and wife... between neighbors, between boss and employee. What can be done? It sounds almost simplistic to say we need to turn to God—but that is the only lasting solution.... Only He can subdue the violence and anger that rage within us, and replace them with His peace and love. Whatever wars rage in your life, lay them at the foot of the Cross and ask Jesus to give you His peace.

AUGUST 5

The story is told of a little girl whose father was an airline pilot. As they crossed the Atlantic, a storm came up.... The little girl opened her eyes, saw the lightning flashing around the plane, and asked, "Is Daddy at the controls?" The flight attendant replied, "Yes, your father is in the cockpit." The little girl smiled, closed her eyes, and went back to sleep. God is at the controls of our lives. Or, rather, He wants to be at the controls.... If we will only relinquish the control of our lives to Him, He will see us safely home.

This is God, our God forever and ever; He will be our guide even to death. PSALM 48:14

MAY 26

What achievement in life is equal to a happy home and rearing successful children who grow up in praise of their parents? Every material goal, even if it is met, will pass away. But the heritage of children is timeless. Our primary responsibility is to be sure our children grow up in homes where God is honored and the love of Christ reigns. Do your children sense that Christ is at the center of your home?

Children are a gift from God; they are His reward. PSALM 127:3 TLB

AUGUST 6

So often when Satan mounts an attack against us we behave as if we were prisoners of war, or worse, conscientious objectors!... God wants us to live victorious lives—lives that are constantly conquering sin. There is only one way to have victory over sin. That is to walk so closely with Christ that sin no longer dominates your life. It becomes the exception rather than the rule.... The Bible says, "Resist the devil and he will flee from you. Draw near to God and He will draw near to you" (James 4:7-8). Is the devil farther away from you today than he was a week ago? If not, why?

MAY 25

The Bible's account about Hezekiah gives us an idea for problem solving: "Hezekiah received the letter from the hand of the messengers, and read it; and Hezekiah went up to the house of the Lord, and spread it before the Lord. Then Hezekiah prayed before the Lord" (2 Kings 19:14-15). Instead of turning to God as a first resource, we so often turn to Him as a last resort. Follow Hezekiah's formula. Turn to God first with your problems, for only He is capable of handling them in a way that will be your best interest—and according to His perfect will.

AUGUST 7

If God eliminated evil by programming us to perform only good acts, we would lose this distinguishing mark—the ability to make choices. We would no longer be free moral agents. We would be reduced to the status of robots.... Robots do not love. God created us with a capacity to love.... Are you using your ability to make decisions wisely—and using it for God?

I have set before you life and death;...
therefore choose life. DEUTERONOMY 30:19

MAY 24

Some scholars think Job may be the oldest book in the Bible. Whether that is true or not, it certainly deals with one of humanity's oldest questions: Why does God allow suffering?... After all (the argument runs), how could a loving and gracious God allow suffering?... The key is to understand the character of God. That is what Job discovered. No, God never gave him a logical, complete answer for his suffering. But through his experience he came to realize that God could be trusted, because He is merciful and loving. And you can trust Him too—not because He always gives us all the answers, but simply because He is God.

AUGUST 8

I have found that the casual Christian has little or no influence for good upon others. Only the Christian who refuses to compromise in matters of honesty, integrity, and morality is bearing an effective witness for Christ.... Only by a life of obedience to the voice of the Spirit, by daily dying to self, by a full dedication to Christ and constant fellowship with Him are we enabled to live a godly life and have a positive influence on this present ungodly world. Is the world changing you...or are you changing the world?

Do not be conformed to this world, but be transformed. ROMANS 12:2

MAY 23

One of the most amazing things in all the Scriptures is how much time Jesus spent in prayer. He had only three years of public ministry, yet He was never too hurried to spend hours in prayer.... How quickly and carelessly, by contrast, we pray.... Jesus pleaded long and repeatedly. It is recorded that He spent entire nights in fervent appeal. No one could have been busier—but He was never too busy for prayer. What keeps you from making prayer a priority in your schedule?

Whatever you ask the Father in My name He will give you. JOHN 16:23

AUGUST 9

St. Francis of Assisi had discovered the secret of happiness when he prayed:

O Divine Master, grant that I may not so much seek

To be consoled as to console,

To be understood but to understand,

To be loved as to love;

For it is in giving that we receive;

It is in pardoning that we are pardoned;

It is in dying that we are born to eternal life!

The opposite of love isn't hate. It's selfishness. Will you ask the Holy Spirit to free your life from selfishness and fill you instead with His love?

MAY 22

The New Testament makes no separation between belief and obedience. They are linked together as one, because if you truly believe, you will truly follow. Trust makes us part of the Kingdom, but our love for God and obedience to His will are the badges of our citizenship in that Kingdom. That is why the Christian life is a happy blend of trust and toil, resting and striving, receiving and doing. God does His part, and we must do ours....

Is any area of your life "off limits" to Christ? Believe—and obey.

*As the body without the spirit is dead, so faith
without works is dead also.* JAMES 2:26

AUGUST 10

Someone has said that the only certainty in life is uncertainty—and it is true. Governments collapse, stock markets plummet, wars destroy, disasters strike, relationships end. As the writer of Hebrews put it, "Here we have no continuing city" (Hebrews 13:14). Yet deep in the human heart is a yearning for security—a yearning that will not go away…. King David knew the secret: "He who dwells in the secret place of the Most High shall abide under the shadow of the Almighty" (Psalm 91:1). Salvation is not an occasional, vague feeling of God's presence. It is actually dwelling with God, secure in His presence forever. Is your security in Christ?

MAY 21

In the familiar story of the Prodigal Son, the young man was not satisfied to be in his father's house with all of his needs met.... He believed the lie that something more exciting was in store for him away from his father. Isn't this how we sometimes behave—even as Christians?.... By thinking this way and acting on it—whether we go as far away as the Prodigal or not—we create our own desperate circumstances.... Fortunately our heavenly Father always hears our cries. Full of repentance is always answered by full forgiveness.... Don't ever—ever—think Satan's way is better than God's way. It never is.

I will be a Father to you, and you shall be My sons and daughters. 2 CORINTHIANS 6:18

AUGUST 11

During Christ's ministry on earth He had no permanent home.... What a contrast to the home He left in order to come to earth—His heavenly home.... Out of love for you and me, He left heaven's glory for earth's misery. But the story doesn't end there. Now He has returned to heaven—and some day we will join Him. Think of it. He wants to share heaven's glory with us!

One evening a little girl was taking a walk with her father. Looking up at the stars she exclaimed, "Daddy, if the wrong side of heaven is so beautiful, what must the right side be like!"

MAY 20

Sometimes God gives His departing saints glimpses of heaven (partly, I believe, to encourage those of us who remain). Just before dying my grandmother sat up in bed, smiled, and said, "I see Jesus, and He has His hand outstretched to me. And there is Ben, and he has both of his eyes and both of his legs." (Ben, my grandfather, had lost an eye and a leg at Gettysburg.) Are you looking forward to that day when you will go to be with Christ, "which is better by far"?

I desire to depart and be with Christ, which is better by far. PHILIPPIANS 1:23 NIV

AUGUST 12

Alexander Maclaren, the distinguished British preacher of another generation, once wrote, "What disturbs us in this world is not trouble, but our opposition to trouble." Put God to the test when troubles come. He won't let you down. In the midst of a painful illness Paul begged God to intervene and take it away. But God replied "My grace is sufficient for you" (2 Corinthians 12:9). It was for Paul, and it will be for you.

We conducted ourselves in the world...by the grace of God. 2 CORINTHIANS 1:12

MAY 19

When we preach justice, it is justice tempered with love....
When we preach atonement for sin, it is atonement necessitated
because of love, provided by love, finished by love.... When we
preach the return of Christ, we are preaching the fulfillment
of love. No matter what sin we have committed, no matter how
black, dirty, shameful, or terrible in may be, God loves us....
The proof? Jesus Christ, God's only Son, went to the Cross for
us. "For God so loved the world that He gave His only begotten
Son, that whoever believes in Him should not perish but have
eternal life" (John 3:16).

AUGUST 13

Jesus ate with publicans and sinners. Nearly everyone He associated with was an outcast.... We are to "weep with those who weep," suffer with those who suffer, and identify ourselves with the poor, the sick, and the needy in body, mind, and spirit. How else can we reach them for Christ? We are to love those who are involved in the world without being contaminated, influenced, or swayed by them. We achieve this distinction only by a close walk with Christ. Like Him, we are to be in the world, but not of the world. It is good for a ship to be in the sea, but bad when the sea gets into the ship.

MAY 18

It's natural to concentrate on what the angels do for us, these who are "sent to serve those who will inherit salvation" (Hebrews 1:14 NIV). But the Bible indicates the angels do much more than that. Especially, we are told, the angels unite in constant praise to God, giving glory to His name and rejoicing in His holiness and perfection.... Are they not examples to us? Shouldn't rejoicing and praise be hallmarks of our lives? Praise will banish darkness, and bring us closer to God. Martin Luther once said, "Come, let us sing a psalm and drive away the devil!"

AUGUST 14

Peace carries with it the idea of unity, completeness, rest, ease, and security. Many times when I meet Jewish friends I greet them with "Shalom," the Hebrew word for peace. And often, when I greet my Arab friends I use a similar term that they use for peace, "Salam."… When you and I yield to worry, we deny our Guide the right to lead us forward in confidence and peace. Don't cause Him to grieve of you by indulging in worry, but trust everything into His all-loving care.

You will keep him in perfect peace, whose mind is stayed on You. ISAIAH 26:3

MAY 17

A police sergeant once asked me the secret of victorious Christian living. I told him there is no magic formula. But if any one word could describe it, it would be surrender. You may ask, "How can I surrender my life?"... There needs to be confession of sin and a complete yielding of every area of our lives, personalities, and wills to Jesus Christ—plus faith that Christ will accept that commitment.... Jesus said, "If anyone desires to come after Me, let him deny himself, and take up his cross daily, and follow Me" (Luke 9:23). Daily surrender—that's the key to daily victory.

AUGUST 15

The first key to usefulness in God's Kingdom is humility. Pride cuts us off from God (and from other people), and deceives us into thinking we can do God's work without God's power.... But there is a second key, and that is faith—faith that God is sovereign, and that He is at work, even if we can't see it. Habakkuk complained to God that evil people were winning that day. But God replied, "I will work a work in your days which you would not believe, though it were told you" (Habakkuk 1:5).... He alone is sovereign—and that is why we can trust Him, even when the way seems dark.

MAY 16

From one end of the Bible to the other, there is the record of those whose prayers were answered—men and women who turned the tide of history by prayer; who fervently prayed, and God answered. Elijah prayed, and God sent fire from heaven to consume the offering on the altar he had built in the presence of God's enemies.... Paul prayed, and dozens of churches were born in Asia Minor and Europe. Peter prayed, and Dorcas was raised to life, to have added years of service for Jesus Christ.... As the seventeenth century theologian, John Owen, said, "He who prays as he ought, will endeavor to live as he prays."

AUGUST 16

To the great gift of forgiveness God adds the great gift of the Holy Spirit. He is the source of power who meets our need to escape from the miserable weakness that grips us. If we are to live a life of sanity in our modern world, if we wish to be men and women who can live victoriously, we need the two-sided gift God has offered us…. As a friend of mine has said, "I just need Jesus Christ for my eternal life, and the Holy Spirit of God for my internal life." He might have added, "…so I can live my external life to the fullest."

MAY 15

I wonder if you've ever thought about the incredible number of messages that rain down on us every day: television ads, e-mails, phone calls, magazines, junk mail, videos, billboards, conversations—the list is almost endless. How many of those shape our thinking?... God says our thinking must be shaped by His truth. What this world calls valuable, God calls worthless. What this world scorns, God exalts.... Jesus said, "You call me Teacher and Lord, and you say well, for so I am" (John 13:13). Is He your Teacher and Lord—or is the world?

AUGUST 17

As Christians, we aren't to isolate ourselves for the world in which we live.... The Old Testament prophets condemned those who ignored the poor and exploited the weak.... As Christians, we know human society is affected by sin, and any effort to improve society will always be incomplete and imperfect. We will never build a Utopia on earth. But we must do all we can to alleviate suffering, and to strike at the root causes of injustice, racial prejudice, hunger, and violence.... Jesus saw the crowds and "was moved with compassion" (Matthew 9:36). Christ is concerned about the whole person—including the society in which that person lives. Do we share His concern?

MAY 14

Years ago Dr. Harold Wolff, professor of medicine at Cornell University Medical College and associate professor of psychiatry, said, "Hope, like faith and a purpose in life, is medicinal. This is not a statement of belief, but a conclusion proved by meticulously controlled scientific experiment." When hope dies, despair will overwhelm us. Hope is both biologically and psychologically vital to us. Men and women must have hope—and true hope comes only from Christ. He gives us hope for the future as we turn in faith to Him—hope for eternity, and hope right now.

My heart is glad, and...my flesh also will rest in hope. PSALM 16:9

AUGUST 18

What is an ambassador? He is a representative and servant of his government in a foreign land. He is not free to set his own policies or develop his own message…in other words, he is a person under authority. In the same way we are called to live under the authority of Jesus Christ and the authority of the Scriptures…. The world today is looking for holy men and women who live under the authority of the Word of God. Unbelievers will not listen to what we say unless we back it up with the way we live. Are you a faithful ambassador for Christ to those around you?

MAY 13

"The supreme happiness of life," Victor Hugo said, "is the conviction that we are loved."... Unfortunately, many people go through life feeling unloved—and unlovable.... No matter the reason, your feelings aren't telling you the truth! God loves you, and if you begin to see yourself the way God sees you, your attitudes will begin to change. If He didn't love you, would Christ have been willing to die for you? But He did! The Bible says, "By this we know love, because He laid down His life for us" (1John 3:16). God loves you. Hammer that truth into your heart and mind every day. It will make all the difference.

AUGUST 19

I once heard a carpenter say that it is always better, and usually more economical, to construct a new house than to patch up an old one. This is even more true in the spiritual realm. The old nature with its deceitfulness, its depravity, and its wickedness must give way to a new nature. And this is exactly what God stands ready to do. God says, "I will give you a new heart and put a new spirit within you" (Ezekiel 36:26).... He wants to remake us completely into the likeness of Christ! He wants to come into our lives and begin to change us from within. Have you asked Him to do that? He will!

MAY 12

Throughout His earthly life, Jesus was constantly exposed to personal criticism and rejection…. How did He respond to criticism and rejection? First, with steadfastness. He did not tone down His message, nor did He stop doing what He knew was right. Second, with strength. Ahead of Him was the Cross—but He did not lose courage or shrink from what He knew was God's will. Third, with submission. When Herod prodded Him to defend Himself, "He answered him nothing" (Luke 23:9). Only one thing mattered: Fulfilling God's purpose for His life. How will we meet criticism?

He is despised and rejected by men,
a Man of sorrows and acquainted with grief.
ISAIAH 53:3

AUGUST 20

A child develops muscles through exercise. Only when our muscles encounter resistance, do they become stronger. In the same way, the Bible tells us that we only become stronger spiritually through exercise—through using our spiritual "muscles" to meet the challenges of life. This is especially true when we face suffering and affliction, for they are one of God's ways to make us strong.... In the last essay he wrote before he died, the great Christian writer C.S. Lewis said, "We have no right to happiness; only an obligation to do our duty." Sometimes our God-given duty will include suffering. When it does, ask God to teach you through it.

MAY 11

No person is meek by nature.... Moses was meek, but he was not meek by nature. God worked meekness into his life over a forty-year period. Peter was certainly not meek by nature. He was impetuous, saying and doing the first thing that came into his mind. But little by little, the Holy Spirit of God transformed Peter after the resurrection of Jesus.... Only the Spirit of God can transform our lives though the new birth experience and then make us over again into the image of Christ. He is our example of true meekness.

The fruit of the Spirit is...gentleness,...
goodness...meekness. GALATIANS 5:22-23 KJV

AUGUST 21

What would you do if you were about to meet the Queen of England? I'm sure you would go out of your way to dress correctly and to be properly briefed.... Some day you and I will meet a far greater Sovereign: The King of the universe.... Our cry will be that of Revelation: "You are worthy, O Lord, to receive glory and honor and power" (Revelation 4:11). Are you prepared for that day when you will meet the King of kings face to face?... The time for you to prepare is now, by committing your life to Christ and beginning to live as a child of the King.

MAY 10

Throughout eternity there will be an intimate relationship between Christ and His church. He will be the Lamb who is in the midst of the throne, and He shall lead them to fountains of living waters. With this great certainty and assurance, the future holds no terrors we cannot face. Beyond the crisis lies heaven and the utopia of our dreams. Thus the Christian should never be filled with fear, discouragement, or despondency. Ahead of us is heaven!

AUGUST 22

A secret agent is one who seeks to protect his country, his king, or his president against evil forces that are opposed to the one he serves.... God has His own secret agents—the angels. Unseen and unrecognized by the world, they never fail in their appointed tasks.

Much has been written recently about angels—often not based on the Bible but on popular legends.... Only in eternity will we know how many accidents they prevented, or how often they kept Satan's malicious spirits at bay. In the meantime, we can take comfort in their presence, and thank God for the love He expresses for us through their service.

MAY 9

The way we use our bodies will signal to others what we really are on the inside. We may claim to follow Christ, but if our actions tell a different story, people have a right to question our claim. Our dress, our speech, our habits—all should honor Christ. We are to be "blameless and pure, children of God without fault in the midst of a crooked and depraved generation" (Philippians 2:15 NIV).

Present your bodies as a living sacrifice....
And be not conformed to this world.
ROMANS 12:1-2 KJV

AUGUST 23

Radio was just coming of age when I was a boy. We would gather around a crude homemade set and twist the tuning dials. Often the only sound was the squeak and squawk of static. It wasn't very exciting, but we kept at it. We knew that…if we established contact, we could hear a voice loud and clear. Does God speak to us? Is He trying to reach us? Yes! The problem is not with Him, but with us. Like that crude radio, we aren't attuned to Him…. God is trying to break through to us—but we must "tune in" to His Word. Are you listening?

MAY 8

Why does Jesus say we should be "pure in heart" (Matthew 5:8)? The reason is because our heart—our inner being—is the root of all our actions. From our hearts come our motives, our desires, our goals, our emotions. If our hearts aren't right, neither will be our actions.... God wants to give us a pure heart—and He will. He does this first of all when we turn to Christ in repentance and faith.... But He does it also day by day, as we submit to the Holy Spirit and—with His help—flee from evil and seek what is good.

AUGUST 24

Only God can meet our deepest yearnings. As St. Augustine said centuries ago, "You have made us for Yourself, O God, and our hearts are restless until they find their rest in You." What crowds out a yearning for God in your life? Don't let anything—or anyone—come between you and God. Isaiah wrote, "Why do you spend money for what is not bread, and your wages for what does not satisfy?" (Isaiah 55:2). God wants you to know Him in a personal way, and He has made this possible through Jesus Christ. He loves you, and He will give you His peace.

MAY 7

When we hear the word suffering we usually think of physical pain. But psychological suffering is just as real—and sometimes more devastating…. Paul knew what it was to experience psychological suffering; he told the Corinthians he had written them "out of much affliction and anguish of heart" (2 Corinthians 2:4). Jesus in the Garden of Gethsemane, "being in agony,…prayed more earnestly" (Luke 22:44). After denying His Lord three times, Peter "went out and wept bitterly" (Luke 22:62).

But when such times come (and they come to us all) God still loves us. He does not abandon us. Remember: "The eternal God is your refuge, and underneath are the everlasting arms" (Deuteronomy 33:27).

AUGUST 25

Only when Paul admitted to his own weakness and was willing to get out of the way, could God take over and work. If we try to do God's will in our own strength, then we can take the credit for whatever gets accomplished.... In the Old Testament God repeatedly told the leaders of Israel to reduce the size of their armies, or He announced in advance how their victory would be won. Why? So they would place their trust in Him and not in their own strength.

When I am weak, then I am strong.

2 CORINTHIANS 12:10

MAY 6

It is a fact that the Lord is my light and my salvation. So why should I be afraid?... God is able, indeed He is anxious, to deliver us from all sorts of trouble. He wants to give us strength to overcome the temptation to sin that separates Him from those He loves. He wants to give us the courage to confront our problems...and then to find the practical wisdom and help we need to deal with them. What do you fear today?... Whatever it is, ask God to help you turn it over to Him. "The Lord is my light and my salvation; whom shall I fear?" (Psalm 27:1).

AUGUST 26

Our Lord regarded His followers as a select company who belonged to a different world from the rest of humanity. Many of the religious people of His day were worldly and unspiritual, publicly parading their religion to impress others while privately dominated by pride, ambition, greed, and falsehood. Jesus told His disciples they could not make their light shine by sinking to the world's low level. It was only by abiding in Christ and living under the ruling power of His Holy Spirit that they could rise above the world. Only in that way could they be salt and light to a decaying and darkened world.

Let your light so shine before men, that they may...glorify your Father in heaven.
MATTHEW 5:16

MAY 5

When a person comes in contact with the living God, he or she can never be the same again. This divine "fire" either draws in or drives away, saves or destroys, helps or hinders. Accepted and utilized, it becomes a boon and a blessing. Rejected, it becomes a bane and a curse. One dying thief was drawn to the warmth of the Savior; he responded in faith and was saved. The other dying thief turned away and rejected God's compassion; he was lost forever.... No, you will never be the same once you know Christ. What difference will He make in your life today?

I will give them a new heart and a new mind.
EZEKIEL 11:19 TEV

AUGUST 27

The Bible reveals that God has a plan for every life, and that if we live in constant fellowship with Him, He will direct and lead us in the fulfillment of this plan.

God does not reveal His plan through fortune-tellers, astrologers, soothsayers, and workers of hocus-pocus. His perfect will is reserved for those who have trusted Christ for salvation. He shares His secrets only with those who are redeemed and transformed, and who humbly seek His will for their lives.... Whatever decisions you face today, commit them to God and ask Him to guide you—and He will.

MAY 4

Thankfulness isn't our usual response when something goes wrong. We may have a hundred good things for which to be thankful—but let one bad thing happen, and it's all we think about! But the Bible says, "in everything give thanks" (1 Thessalonians 5:18). No matter what happens, we are to give thanks. Cultivate a spirit of thanksgiving in your life. Thank God for every blessing He gives you. Thank Him for Christ and what He has done for you. Even when things go wrong, thank Him that they aren't worse, and you are still in His hands.

Let the peace of Christ rule in your hearts....
And be thankful. Colossians 3:15 niv

AUGUST 28

Walking always implies movement, progress, direction. This is what it means to walk with God. It means moving forward in step with Him, confident that the way He is leading is best. The problem is that we are weak.... But that is one reason why the Holy Spirit has been given to us. Galatians 5:16 could be paraphrased this way: "Walk by means of the Spirit," One of the highest commendations in the Bible is found in these words about Noah: "Noah was a just man, perfect in his generations. Noah walked with God" (Genesis 6:9). Could this be said of us?

MAY 3

Years ago when I traveled to Europe to preach I liked to travel by sea, to enjoy the five days of relative quiet on the ship. On one of my voyages Captain Anderson of the United States took me down to see the ship's gyroscope. He said, "When the sea is rough, the gyroscope helps to keep the ship on an even keel…." As I listened, I thought how like the gyroscope is the Holy Spirit in our hearts…. Our souls will be kept on an even keel and in perfect peace with the Holy Spirit dwells in our hearts. He comforts us with God's abiding presence, and assures us that God's promises are true.

AUGUST 29

As a boy I grew up in the rural American South. My idea of the ocean was so small that the first time I saw the Atlantic I couldn't comprehend how any lake could be so big! The vastness of the ocean cannot be understood until it is seen. This is the same with God's love. It passes knowledge. Until you actually experience it, no one can describe its wonders to you.... No matter what comes your way...no matter how tempted you are to give in to despair...never forget: God's love for you can never be exhausted, for His love is beyond measure.

MAY 2

We Christians should stand out like sparkling diamonds against a dark velvet background. We should be more wholesome than anyone else. We should be poised, cultured, courteous, gracious—but firm in the things we do or do not do.... The Bible says, "Those who are wise will shine like the brightness of the heavens, and those who lead many to righteousness, like the stars for ever and ever" (Daniel 12:3 NIV). Dr. Albert Schweitzer, the great missionary doctor and statesman, once said, "To be glad instruments of God's love in this imperfect world is the service to which man is called."

AUGUST 30

At any one time at least thirty wars rage in various parts of the world, in addition to countless instances of civil unrest.... In the midst of an uncertain and threatening world, however, we can have peace. It comes from putting our trust in the living God. Isaiah's words—written in a time of great upheaval—still speak to us today: "Those who wait on the Lord shall renew their strength;...they shall walk and not faint" (Isaiah 40:31).

MAY 1

Television sets pull in hundreds of channels;...millions of people own second and third homes for vacations; our children are upset if they don't get the latest computer games for Christmas.... Down inside is an empty place in our hearts... that will not go away. The irony is, the more we try to satisfy it, the less content we become. Only Christ can fill that empty space in our hearts, and He will as we open our lives to Him. But God's Word also points us to the future—to heaven, where our restless hearts will be at peace. "There remains, therefore, a rest for the people of God" (Hebrews 4:9).

AUGUST 31

Movie marquees, the covers of magazines, the Internet, billboards, television—all scream sensual messages at us. "If it feels good, do it" has become a national motto. Yet, if you talk with people who have come to Christ out of deep sin, they will tell you they wish they had never fallen into such sin, and that they had come to Christ sooner.... The secret of purity is God. When we are committed to Christ, we will shrink back from all that is impure. Instead, we will seek a pure heart—a heart cleansed by the Holy Spirit and the Word of God.

You shall be holy, for I the Lord your God am holy. LEVITICUS 19:2

APRIL 30

Jesus, we read, "having risen a long while before daylight...went out and departed to a solitary place; and there He prayed" (Mark 1:35). If the Son of God needed time alone with His Father, how much more do we? It is not easy to shut out the world, set aside a few minutes by yourself, and spend time in God's Word and prayer. But it is essential if we are to grow in our relationship with God and be strengthened for the battles ahead. Don't delay. Begin now to spend time alone with God every day.

SEPTEMBER 1

In North Carolina I have visited the textile mills and have watched the giant looms that turn out cloth for the nation. The shuttles move with the speed of lightning, scarcely visible to the naked eye. Job says that his days are "swifter than a weaver's shuttle." Life passes so quickly it is almost over before we realize it. The Bible says this is the chronology of eternity. Though you live to be seventy, eighty, or ninety years old, that is but a snap of the finger compared to eternity.... We have only a few brief years at the most. Let's live them for the Lord.

APRIL 29

Becoming a Christian is a once-for-all event, in which we repent of our sins and cast ourselves on Christ alone for our salvation. When we are converted, God takes us "out of darkness into His marvelous light" (1 Peter 2:9). But being a Christian... is a lifelong process of daily repentance and faith, turning from sin and seeking to live for Christ, in the power of the Holy Spirit.... Although we have been converted and God has come to live in us, our old nature is still "alive and kicking." Our stubborn wills still demand to put self first instead of Christ.... Who will control your will today? You—or Christ?

SEPTEMBER 2

As we trust in Christ, God gives us the Spirit as a pledge, or, as some translations read, earnest or guarantee. "He...put his Spirit in our hearts as a deposit, guaranteeing what is to come" (2 Corinthians 1:21-22 NIV). In the apostle Paul's day, a deposit or pledge did three things: It was a down payment that sealed a bargain, it represented an obligation to buy, and it was a sample of what was to come.... The Holy Spirit in our hearts is God's pledge or deposit to us—sealing His commitment to save us, guaranteeing that some day our salvation will be complete, and enabling us to experience its joys right now.

APRIL 28

Many Christians do not see God in all of His wholeness. We glibly quote John 3:16—but we forget the following verses: "He who does not believe has been judged already" (verse 18 NASB). Yes, God is loving and compassionate. But He is also absolutely holy and pure…. Sin is an offense to Almighty God, and while He will have mercy on us when we repent, He also is the Judge, and "everything is uncovered and laid bare before the eyes of Him to whom we must give account" (Hebrews 4:13 NIV).

SEPTEMBER 3

In a society of unredeemed people, democracy is the only fair and equitable system. But no democracy can ever be better than the people who make it up. When citizens are selfishly motivated, the government will be inequitable. When people are dishonest, the government will be the same. When everyone wants his own way, someone is going to get hurt. But in God's kingdom, Christ is King. He is compassionate, fair, merciful, and just. When He is sovereign in men's hearts, anguish turns to peace, hatred is transformed into love, and misunderstanding into harmony. Is Christ the King of your motives and your attitudes?

APRIL 27

Amidst the world's confusion, God's omnipotent hand moves, working out His unchanging plan and purpose…. By His providence He sustains us, and behind the scenes He is working to bring about His divine purpose. What is that purpose? Paul recorded it this way: "That…He might gather together in one all things in Christ, both which are in heaven and which are on earth" (Ephesians 1:10)…. Some day all the sin and rebellion of this corrupted universe will be destroyed, and Christ's kingdom of righteousness and peace will rule forever. Don't be discouraged by what you see in the headlines every day. God is at work, and some day Christ will rule.

SEPTEMBER 4

I wonder how many of us will look back over a lifetime of wasted opportunities and ineffective witness, and weep because we did not allow God to use us as He wanted. "Night is coming, when no man can work" (John 9:4 NASB). If ever we are to study the Scriptures, if ever we are to spend time in prayer, if ever we are to win souls for Christ, if ever we are to invest our finances for His kingdom—it must be now.

You do not know what will happen tomorrow. JAMES 4:14

APRIL 26

Heaven is a place so beautiful that when John, the Apostle, caught a glimpse of it, the only thing to which he could liken it was a young woman on the crowning day of her life: her wedding day (Revelation 21:2).... Yet the Bible's emphasis is not on heaven's beauty but on heaven's joy. The Bible teaches that heaven will be a home that is happy because there will be nothing in it to hinder happiness. "There shall by no means enter it anything that defiles.... But the throne of God and of the Lamb shall be in it" (Revelation 21:27; 22:3).

SEPTEMBER 5

To the Christian, death is said in the Bible to be a coronation. The picture here is that of a regal prince who, after his struggles and conquests in an alien land, returns to his native country and court to be crowned and honored for his deeds.... When D.L. Moody was dying, he looked up to heaven and said, "Earth is receding, heaven is opening, this is my coronation day."

There is laid up for me a crown of righteousness, which the Lord, the righteous Judge, will give to me on that Day.
2 TIMOTHY 4:8

APRIL 25

Charles Allen once made this statement: "Some people seem to have such a passion for righteousness that they have no room left for compassion for those who have failed."

I pray that would never be true of us. God, our Father, has shown us great kindness and gentle mercy. May we ever reach out to the lost in compassion and love to bring them gently to Jesus Christ. Jesus, "when He saw the multitudes,…was moved with compassion for them, because they were weary and scattered, like sheep having no shepherd" (Matthew 9:36).

SEPTEMBER 6

Walk with God as Moses did in the solitude of the desert; when the hour of judgment fell upon Egypt, Moses was prepared to lead his people to victory.... Walk with God as Daniel and his three young friends did in the palace of Babylon's king; when the fiery furnace and the lion's den came, God was beside them and delivered them.... God has not promised to deliver us from trouble, but He has promised to go with us through the trouble. "Yea, though I walk through the valley of the shadow of death, I will fear no evil; for You are with me" (Psalm 23:4).

APRIL 24

We live in an age when sin is winked at and where God is treated as one who is indulgent, softhearted, and understanding—tolerant of those who break His commandments.... But I will tell you that God has not forgotten about sin.... God hates sin. Why? Because He loves us, and He knows the terrible devastation sin brings to us. Sin is like a deadly cancer, inexorably bringing suffering and death in its wake. Left unforgiven, sin also sends men and women into a timeless eternity apart from God—into Hell.... Confess your sin today. Don't wait. Receive from God's forgiveness and restoration so that you might be of use to Him and enjoy His love forever.

SEPTEMBER 7

It is an undeniable fact that usually those who have suffered most are best able to comfort others who are passing through suffering. They know what it is to suffer, and they understand more than others what a suffering person is experiencing—physically, emotionally, and spiritually…. Our attitude toward suffering should not be, "Grit your teeth and bear it," hoping it will pass as quickly as possible. Rather, our goal should be to learn all we can from what we are called upon to endure, so that we in turn can "comfort each other and edify one another" (1 Thessalonians 5:11).

APRIL 23

Only surrendered Christians will make an impact on our world. The world does not need any more lukewarm Christians, or lazy Christians, or quarrelsome Christians, or doubting Christians, or prideful Christians. The Bible says, "a double minded man is unstable in all his ways" (James 1:8 KJV). What keeps you from a full surrender of your life to the King of kings and the Lord of lords? Your response will make the difference between success and failure in your spiritual life. It will make the difference between your needing help and being able to help others.... This is the Christian's hour of decision!

SEPTEMBER 8

The promised coming of Christ has been the great hope of believers down through the centuries. The ancient Nicene Creed affirms, "He shall come again with glory."

Charles Wesley wrote 7,000 hymns; 5,000 mention the coming of Christ. As the Archbishop of Canterbury crowned Queen Elizabeth II, he stated, "I give thee, O Sovereign Lady, this crown to wear until He who reserves the right to wear it shall return."... Some day the heavens will shout, "The kingdoms of this world have become the kingdoms of our Lord and of His Christ, and He shall reign forever and ever!" (Revelation 11:15). Christ alone is the answer to the burdens of our hearts and the hopelessness of our world.

APRIL 22

Do you remember the violent storm that came upon Jesus and His disciples one night on the Sea of Galilee? His disciples grew panicky—but Jesus stayed fast asleep. He was at peace because He knew God was in control. He was at peace also because He was sovereign over the storm, and He knew it would vanish at His Word: "Peace, be still!" (Mark 4:39). His Word still calms the turmoil in our lives. Is some storm making you fearful today? Stay close to Jesus, for His Word brings peace.

May the God of hope fill you with all joy and peace. ROMANS 15:13

SEPTEMBER 9

I was reared in a small Presbyterian church in Charlotte, North Carolina. Before I was ten years of age my mother made me memorize the "Shorter Catechism," a summary of basic Christian beliefs in the form of questions and answers. In the catechism we were asked to define God. The answer we learned was, "God is a Spirit—infinite, eternal, and unchangeable." Those three words beautifully describe God. He is infinite—not body-bound. Eternal—He has no beginning and no ending. He is unchangeable—never changing, never capricious, never unreliable.... His love never changes. His holiness never changes. His purpose never changes.... Can you think of any reason not to trust Him? Neither can I!

APRIL 21

Once many years ago when I was going through a dark period...I felt as though God had disappeared and that I was alone in my trial and burden.... I wrote my mother about the experience and will never forget her reply: "Son, there are many times when God withdraws to test your faith. He wants you to trust Him in the darkness. Now, Son, reach up by faith in the fog and you will find that His hand will be there." In tears I knelt by my bed and experienced an overwhelming sense of God's presence. Whether or not we feel God's presence when our way seems dark, by faith we know He is there. You can stake your life on His promise: "I will never leave you nor forsake you" (Hebrews 13:5).

SEPTEMBER 10

The Christian faith brings its own "blood, sweat, and tears" to those who would follow Jesus Christ.... So are we simply exchanging one burden for another—the burden of sin for the burden of obedience? No! It is no burden to follow Christ. Instead, we become the bearers of joy—because now we are yoked to the very Son of God. Nor is it too heavy to bear, for Christ bears it with us: "My yoke is easy and My burden is light" (Matthew 11:30). With whom are you yoked—the world or Christ?

Take My yoke upon you and learn from Me.
MATTHEW 11:29

APRIL 20

September 11 will be engraved on the memories of people everywhere for generations to come. On that terrible day when terrorists commanded several passenger planes and killed thousands of innocent people in New York and Washington, we began to realize the true depths of evil in the human heart, and the uncertainty and fragility of life itself. What lessons would God teach us from such an appalling tragedy? I confess I don't know the full answer.... Life has always been uncertain; September 11 only made it clearer. Where will you turn for your security? Put your life in Christ's hands, for only He offers us "a kingdom which cannot be shaken" (Hebrews 12:28).

SEPTEMBER 11

Our influence on society depends on our likeness to Jesus Christ. We cannot elevate others higher than we ourselves have gone. The first century Christians out-thought, out-lived, and out-loved their neighbors, and by their example of purity and compassion attracted countless thousands to the Christian faith. What do others see in your life that would attract them to Christ?

Let your light so shine before men, that
they may...glorify your Father in heaven.
MATTHEW 5:16

APRIL 19

The Bible tells us that our lives are heaven's primary concern…. Think of it: Even the angels of heaven are constantly watching how we live as Christians!… They know the hour is urgent and that what we do is important. Eternal issues are at stake, and we are in the midst of a cosmic struggle. Don't think it doesn't matter how you live; it does! It matters to God, and it matters to His holy angels. It also matters to those around you. Jesus said, "Let your light so shine before men, that they may see your good works and glorify your Father in heaven" (Matthew 5:16).

SEPTEMBER 12

One lesson that Jesus would teach us is to have confidence that God answers every true petition. Skeptics may question it, humanists may deny it, and intellectuals may ridicule it. Yet here is Christ's own promise: "If you abide in me, and My words abide in you, you will ask what you desire, and it shall be done for you" (John 15:7).... Does He promise to give us anything we want, if we just keep asking? No. God loves us too much to answer prayers that are foolish or might harm us.... The Bible promises, "No good thing does he withhold from those whose walk is blameless" (Psalm 84:11 NIV). Trust that promise with all your soul.

APRIL 18

Corrie ten Boom once explained, "Picture a piece of embroidery placed between you and God, with the right side up toward God. Man sees the loose, frayed ends; but God sees the pattern." God is in control. Whatever comes into our lives, we can confidently say, "We know that all things work together for good to those who love God, to those who are called according to His purpose" (Romans 8:28).

SEPTEMBER 13

Some years ago, a woman wrote me that she had pleaded for ten years for the conversion of her husband, but that he was more hardened than ever. I advised her to continue to plead. Sometime later I heard from her again. She said her husband was gloriously and miraculously converted in the eleventh year of her prayer vigil. How thankful she was that she had kept on praying! The Scripture says, "Pray without ceasing" (1 Thessalonians 5:17).... Your responsibility isn't to tell God when He must act or even how He must act. Your responsibility is simply to "pray without ceasing," trusting Him to act according to His perfect will.

APRIL 17

Christians are warned not to love the world—but what is worldliness?... It is an attitude that puts self first and ignores God and His commandments.... We must avoid everything God has labeled as sinful; of that there can be no doubt. But some elements of daily life aren't necessarily sinful in themselves; they only become sinful if they are abused. Pleasure isn't always wrong—unless it is abused. Ambition is an essential part of true character—but if abused it can destroy us. Be on guard, lest a spirit of worldliness creep into your life. The Bible warns, "Do not love the world, or the things in the world."

SEPTEMBER 14

As Mary looked into the tomb she saw "two angels in white sitting, one at the head and the other at the feet, where the body of Jesus had lain" (John 20:12). Then one of the angels who was sitting outside the tomb proclaimed the greatest message the world had ever heard: "He is not here; for He is risen" (Matthew 28:6). Those few words changed the history of the universe. Darkness and despair died; hope and anticipation were born in the hearts of men.... Don't leave Jesus at the manger...or on the Cross...or in the tomb. He is alive and even now He wants to walk beside you every day.

APRIL 16

The Bible has scores of references telling us how much it pleases God for us to trust Him for every need.... Jesus told His disciples, "Look at the birds...they neither sow nor reap nor gather into barns; yet your heavenly Father feeds them. Are you not of more value than they?" (Matthew 6:26). God values our trust in Him above every other character quality. And how do we develop trust? By spending time in God's presence, through prayer, worship, and reading His Word. We develop it also as we step out in faith, and discover He really can be trusted. Are you trusting Him for every need in your life?

SEPTEMBER 15

The angel who came to the garden where Jesus' body lay, rolled away the stone and permitted fresh air and morning light to fill His tomb. The sepulcher was no longer an empty vault or dreary mausoleum; rather it was a life-affirming place that radiated the glory and power of the living God.... An unknowing poet has said of the tomb, "'Tis now a cell where angels used to come and go with heavenly news." No words of men or angels can adequately describe the height and depth, the length and breadth of the glory to which the world awakened when Jesus came forth to life from the pall of death.

APRIL 15

Christians don't fail to live as they should because they are in the world; they fail because the world has gotten into them. We don't fail to produce the fruit of the Holy Spirit because we live in a sea of corruption; we fail because the sea of corruption has gotten into us.... Most ocean-going ships have pumps running constantly, sucking out any water that might have leaked into the hull. Similarly, we need to keep the "pumps" of repentance running. We need to plug the holes with the truth of God's Word. Don't let the world sink your ship!

SEPTEMBER 16

There is no possibility of true happiness until we have established friendship and fellowship with God. And there is no possibility of establishing this fellowship apart from the Cross of His Son, Jesus Christ. God says, "I will forgive you, but I will forgive only at the foot of the Cross." He says, "I will fellowship with you, but I will fellowship with you only at the Cross." Why is this? Because only through Christ's death on the Cross can we be forgiven and reconciled to God.... It is as if an accounting entry had been made in the books of heaven, declaring us righteous for Christ's sake. The Divine Bookkeeper cancels our debt!

APRIL 14

Some section hands on a British railroad found a thrush's nest under the rail and the hen peacefully sitting on the eggs, undisturbed by the roar of the fast trains above and around her. What a picture of perfect trust! The Bible says, "You will keep him in perfect peace, whose mind is stayed on You" (Isaiah 26:3). Believe me, God's grace is more than adequate for these times. Even as I grow older, I am learning, day by day, to keep my mind centered on Christ. When we do, the worries and anxieties and concerns of the world pass away and nothing but "perfect peace" is left in the human heart.

SEPTEMBER 17

We can never grasp the horror of human sin until we realize it caused the Son of God to be crucified. Not Pilate, not Judas, not the mob—but sin.... The terrible bitter cup of humanity's sin sent Him to the Cross. Jesus prayed in those last hours, "O, My Father, if it is possible, let this cup pass from Me; nevertheless, not as I will, but as You will" (Matthew 26:39).... Why did He drink that awful cup? So you and I would not have to. Sin is the second most powerful force in the universe, for it sent Jesus to the Cross. Only one force is greater—the love of God.

APRIL 13

A prayer does not have to be eloquent or contain the language and terms of a theologian. In fact, sometimes our simplest, most heartfelt prayers are the most pleasing to God…. My wife has a notebook she has kept of our children as they were beginning to talk. She treasures these first attempts, mistakes and all. She said, "I wouldn't take anything for that book." When Paul said we should "pray without ceasing" (1 Thessalonians 5:17) he chose a term used in his day to describe a persistent cough…. God is interested in everything we do, and nothing is too great or too insignificant to share with Him.

SEPTEMBER 18

One of the great hymns of the church, "The Solid Rock," by Edward Mote and William Bradbury, begins, "My hope is built on nothing less, than Jesus' blood and righteousness."... On what is your hope built? You may hope for a raise in pay at work. You may hope that you pass an exam at school. You may even hope that you win a contest you have entered.... But all these "hopes" fade into insignificance when compared with the greatest hope of all—our hope of salvation in Christ. And that hope is an absolute certainty, because it is based not on ourselves or our good works, but squarely on "Jesus' blood and righteousness."

APRIL 12

The Bible is more modern than tomorrow's newspaper. It says the consummation of all things shall be the coming again of Jesus Christ to this earth. This truth gives us hope—but it should also sober us and make us more diligent.... Jesus Himself said, "Of that day and hour no one knows, not even the angels of heaven, but My Father only" (Matthew 24:36). Believing in the return of Christ doesn't make us less concerned about this world; it makes us more concerned, because we know time may be short. Now is the time to live for Christ and witness for Him.

SEPTEMBER 19

The resurrection of Jesus Christ is the key to God's plan for the future. Unless Christ was raised from the dead, there can be no future kingdom and no returning King. Unless Christ was raised from the dead, sin and death still reign, and God's plan of redemption remains unfulfilled. But Christ has been raised! As the disciples stood watching after Jesus ascended into the heavens, the angels assured them that the risen Christ would some day be the returning Christ.... Just as surely as Christ rose from the dead, so He will return and take us to Himself. Every promise—without exception—will be fulfilled.

APRIL 11

I have known many outstanding leaders who made the Bible their guide. Businessman Herbert J. Taylor, former president of Rotary International, told me he began each day by reading the Sermon on the Mount aloud. Let the Bible be your firm foundation. Let it be the staff of life that nourishes your soul. Let it be the sword of the Spirit that cuts away sin. Many years ago I heard these words: "Sin will keep you from God's Word— or God's Word will keep you from sin!"

All Scripture is given by inspiration of God, and is profitable for doctrine, for reproof, for correction, for instruction in righteousness.

2 TIMOTHY 3:16

SEPTEMBER 20

The message of Easter is the central focus of Christianity. The apostle Paul said, "If Christ has not been raised, your faith is futile; you are still in your sins" (1 Corinthians 15:17 NIV). It is as simple as that. If Christ is still dead, then He cannot be our Savior, for He was not the Son of God, and He died like all men. More than that, heaven's doors are still locked. But if Christ is risen, as the Scriptures teach and as hundreds of witnesses testified…then we have the ultimate hope of humanity—eternal life with the God who made us and the certainty of life beyond the grave.

APRIL 10

"Blessed be the God and father of our Lord Jesus Christ... who comforts us in all our tribulation, that we may be able to comfort those who are in any trouble, with the comfort with which we ourselves are comforted by God" (2 Corinthians 1:3-4).... This passage from Paul suggests a new insight into suffering. Briefly put, it is this: Not only are we comforted in our trials, but our trials can equip us to comfort others. Has God taught you something through your trials that could help someone else today?

SEPTEMBER 21

Note four things about Jesus, the Good Shepherd. He owns the sheep; they belong to Him. Next, He guards the sheep; He never abandons them when danger approaches. Also, He knows the sheep; He calls them by name and they follow Him. Finally, He lays down His life for the sheep; their salvation is His primary concern.

The Bible says, "We are His people and the sheep of His pasture" (Psalm 100:3). Because we belong to Christ, we can be secure and at rest.

I am the good shepherd. JOHN 10:11 NIV

APRIL 9

Once when I referred to the future that God is planning, a university student asked me, "Isn't this a form of escapism?" I said, "In a sense, yes; and before the devil gets through with this world, we are all going to be looking for exit signs!"... The world remains mired in the same heartaches and injustices it has suffered since the Fall—and Jesus said we shouldn't be surprised: "In the world you will have tribulation."... But that isn't the full story! Jesus added, "But be of good cheer, I have overcome the world" (John 16:33). Notice: He not only will overcome the world—He already has!

SEPTEMBER 22

Martha, over-concerned with her workaday duties, said to Jesus, "Lord, do You not care?" How many faithful, loving mothers, overwhelmed by the burdens of motherhood, have cried anxiously, "Lord, do You not care?" That question is forever answered in those reassuring words of Peter: "He cares for you" (1 Peter 5:7). This is the Word of God. Even if the world passes away it will not change. You can be confident God cares for you. If He didn't, would He have sent Christ into the world to die for you? Of course not! That is why you can always turn to Him for the strength and encouragement you need.

APRIL 8

Just as our bodies need food, so our souls need spiritual food. Without it we become malnourished and weak, susceptible to every temptation and unable to do the work God calls us to do. Where do we find this spiritual food? In the Bible, the Word of God. The Bible reveals Christ, the Bread of Life and the Water of Life.... Don't be content to skim through a chapter, merely to satisfy your conscience or because of some long-established habit.... Meditate on it, memorize it, hide it in your heart so it permeates your whole being. A small portion well digested is of far greater spiritual value than a lengthy passage scanned hurriedly.

SEPTEMBER 23

The Bible teaches that blessings follow those who give liberally. Proverbs 11:25 says, "The generous soul will be made rich, and he who waters will also be watered himself."

I've heard countless testimonies from men and women who were afraid to put to the test God's promise to bless those who are generous. They feared they would not have enough. Then, when at last they decided to tithe (to give a tenth of their income) in accordance with the Bible's standard, they began to prosper. They discovered what countless others have known across the ages: You can't out-give God. What keeps you from being more generous in supporting God's work?

APRIL 7

God has revealed Himself. He is not hidden! He has spoken to us, and if we will listen, we can not only discover what He is like, but we can come to know Him in a personal way.… God has two textbooks. One is the "textbook" of nature. By looking at the world, we can learn something about its Creator. The other is the "textbook" of revelation, the Bible. It is more than an ancient record of events; it is God's Word, given to us by the inspiration of the Holy Spirit to guide our lives. God has spoken—and He still speaks. Are you listening?

SEPTEMBER 24

The Bible reminds us that our days are as grass. For a brief time we flourish, but soon we wither and die. Yet the minutes of our lives can be flecked with the gold of eternity. Instead of wasting them—as we so easily do—God exhorts us to redeem the time.

But our lives are also immortal. God made us different from the other creatures. He made us in His own image, a living soul. Don't let anyone tell you that we are simply a higher species of animal. If you believe that, you will begin to act like one. No! You are far greater.

APRIL 6

Jesus said to His disciples: "Do not lay up for yourselves treasures on earth...but lay up for yourselves treasures in heaven.... For where your treasure is, there your heart will be also" (Matthew 6:19-21). Does that mean we must renounce everything we own? No, not unless God clearly commands us to do so. But it does mean we commit everything we have—including our lives—to Christ, and put His will above everything else.

SEPTEMBER 25

God's love did not begin at Calvary. Before the morning stars sang together, before the world was baptized with the first light, before the first blades of grass peeped out, God was love.... Before the worlds were created, He knew all about us and the need we would have some day for Christ to die for us. So in His love "He chose us in him before the creation of the world" (Ephesians 1:4 NIV). God does not change—and neither does His love.... He will love you forever. Will you love Him in return?

APRIL 5

Faith must have an object. We don't simply have faith; we have faith in something or someone.... The Bible says, "Through Him [you] believe in God, who raised Him from the dead and gave Him glory, so that your faith and hope are in God" (1 Peter 1:21). People today put their faith in all kinds of ideas and beliefs, from astrology to alleged "spiritual guides" to science and humanism. But only Christ reveals God to us, and only He can bridge the gap between us and God—a gap caused by sin. Do not be deceived or misled. Only Christ is worthy of your faith.

SEPTEMBER 26

Affliction can be a means of refining and of purification.... We might never have had the songs of Fanny Crosby had she not been afflicted with blindness. George Matheson would never have given the world his immortal song, "O Love that Will Not Let Me Go," had it not been for the pain of personal tragedy and heartache. The "Hallelujah Chorus" was written by Handel when he was poverty-stricken and suffering from a paralyzed right side and right arm.... Whatever the reason, if God sends affliction your way, take it in faith as a blessing, not a curse.

APRIL 4

You aren't saved by your feelings; you are saved by Christ.... The Bible says, "God has given us eternal life, and this life is in His Son. He who has the Son has life" (1 John 5:11-12). That is God's promise to you—and He cannot lie. Your feelings will lie to you—and Satan may even use them to convince you God has abandoned you or that you have lost your salvation.... How wonderful to know our faith is based on God's truth, and not our feelings!

SEPTEMBER 27

Because Christ rose from the dead, we know there is life after death, and that if we belong to Him we need not fear death or hell. Jesus...promised, "If I go and prepare a place for you, I will come back and take you to be with me that you also may be where I am" (John 14:3 NIV). How hopeless our lives would be if these words were not true. Every cemetery and every grave site would be a mute witness to the futility and despair of human life. But His words are true!... What a glorious hope we have because Jesus is alive!

APRIL 3

The death of the righteous is no accident. Do you think that God—whose watchful vigil notes the sparrow's fall and who knows the number of hairs on our heads—would turn His back on one of His children in the hour of peril? With Him there are no accidents, no tragedies, and no catastrophes as far as His children are concerned. It was Sir Walter Scott who asked, "Is death the last sleep? No, it is the final awakening." That is true for every believer in Christ. Even when grief overwhelms us or confusion assails us, we still can trust God's all-knowing love.

SEPTEMBER 28

The apostle Paul, who was a splendid example of a disciplined Christian, said, "I beseech you therefore, brethren, by the mercies of God, that you present your bodies a living sacrifice, holy, acceptable unto God, which is your reasonable service" (Romans 12:1 KJV). If we have given ourselves to Christ, then He has come to live within us, and our bodies are now temples—the dwelling places—of the Holy Spirit.... We must pray as Jeremy Taylor once prayed, "Let my body be a servant of my spirit, and both body and spirit servants of Jesus."

APRIL 2

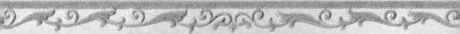

With the exception of Jesus, no one in the Bible probably endured more scorn than Noah…. Can you imagine what his neighbors said? Can you picture them…murmuring he must be out of his mind?… But when the flood came, only Noah and his family were saved. For those who scorned his pleas, it was too late. You and I are called to proclaim a message that often seems foolishness to an unbelieving world—the message of the Cross. Will everyone accept it? No. Will some mock us? Yes. But never stop sharing the Gospel, for it is still "the power of God for the salvation of everyone who believes" (Romans 1:16 NIV).

SEPTEMBER 29

Jesus gave His head to the crown of thorns for us. He gave His face to the human spittle for us. He gave His cheek and His beard to be plucked out for us.... He gave His blood for us. Jesus Christ, dying in our place, taking our sins on that cross, is God's love in action. But that's not the end of the story.... If Christ is not alive, there is no hope for any of us. But He is alive! And because He is, "He is able to save completely those who come to God through Him, because He always lives to intercede for them" (Hebrews 7:25 NIV). Hallelujah!

APRIL 1

The root of discouragement is unbelief.... Discouragement is Satan's device to thwart the work of God in our lives. Discouragement blinds our eyes to the mercy of God and makes us perceive only the unfavorable circumstances. There is only one way to dispel discouragement, and it is not in our own strength or ingenuity. It is to turn in faith to God, believing that He loves us and is in control of the future. The Bible says, "Wait on the Lord...and He shall strengthen your heart" (Psalm 27:14).

SEPTEMBER 30

When Jesus lifted up His voice and cried, "It is finished," He did not mean His life was ebbing away or God's plan had been foiled. Though death was near, Jesus realized the last obstacle had been hurdled and the last enemy destroyed. He had successfully and triumphantly completed the task of redemption. With the words, "It is finished," He announced that heaven's door was open.

He was wounded for our transgressions.
Isaiah 53:5

MARCH 31

The key to understanding tragedy is to understand its source....
When Adam and Eve sinned in the Garden of Eden...it was a
blatant, open act of rebellion—in thought, word, and deed—
against the God who had made them and had supplied their
every need.... Every graveyard, every hospital, every prison,
every courtroom is a witness to the terrible legacy of that
rebellion. No, I don't fully understand why God allows evil
to happen. But evil happens because we live in an evil world.
Never underestimate the devastating effects of sin.... But Christ
triumphed over tragedy—and so can we, because of Him.

OCTOBER 1

When Jesus Christ was on the Cross, His blood draining the life from His body, He knew what it was like to be alone and wracked with pain. But Jesus' pain was far more than just physical pain, for He was suffering God's judgment on all the sins of the ages—the greatest darkness of the soul ever known…. He died in our place…. There was no other way for sin's penalty to be paid, and for us to be redeemed. The Cross is the measure of God's love. How will you respond to His love, poured out on the Cross for you?

MARCH 30

One of the hardest truths for some people to accept is that there is absolutely nothing they can do to win their salvation. No matter how generous...how honest...how compassionate they are—it is never enough.... Only when we see ourselves as God sees us—sinners, guilty before Him—will we realize our need of a Savior.... But the amazing thing is this: In spite of our sin, God still loves us.... All we can do is believe and receive—believe Christ died for us and by faith receive Him into our lives. No, you can't win your salvation—but Christ has won it for you!

OCTOBER 2

When Samuel Morse, inventor of the telegraph, sent his first message, he telegraphed these words: "What hath God wrought!" The greatest news ever sent tells of a far greater event God has wrought: Christ is risen…. When Adam and Eve first sinned, God's warning became a reality: "You shall surely die" (Genesis 2:17). From that moment on, death reigned over the human race—and with it fear, dread, and superstition. But Christ's resurrection changed all that, bringing hope and salvation to all who put their trust in Him. Listen: Death is a defeated foe! Christ has won the victory…. Is your confidence in Jesus Christ, the risen Lord?

MARCH 29

Frequently people say to me, "God answered my prayer!" Usually they mean God granted them whatever they had requested, either for themselves or for others.

God always answers the prayers of His children—but His answer isn't always "Yes." Sometimes His answer is "No," or "Wait"—and they are answers just as much as "Yes."

Think of Paul, pleading with God to remove his "thorn in the flesh" (probably a painful illness). But God's answer was "No" (see 2 Corinthians 12:7-10). God has something better—a path leading him into deeper dependence on God and His grace…. Thank God even when He says "No" or "Wait." His answer is always perfect.

OCTOBER 3

Science has confirmed what the Bible taught centuries ago: There is a close relationship between our minds and bodies.... Guilt, fear, jealousy, bitterness, futility, escapism—these and a host of other problems are spiritual ills, brought about by the disease of sin.... But when Christ comes into our lives, He removes our guilt and takes away our fears. He gives us love for others and a new purpose in life. His joy and peace neutralize sin's poison—and that promotes emotional and physical health. Does that mean our emotional and physical problems will vanish? Not necessarily. But like a spring of pure water, God's peace in our hearts brings cleansing and refreshment to our minds and bodies.

MARCH 28

Things didn't always work out the way Paul planned.... But in every instance God was in control! Paul was forbidden to preach in Asia Minor—because God was opening the door to Europe. Paul found himself in jail—and as a result the Philippian jailer and his family were converted. Paul had to flee Thessalonica—and Berea, the next town, "received the word with all readiness" (Acts 17:11). Things don't always work out the way we plan. But if we commit our way to Christ and walk in obedience to Him, we discover His plans are always better.

As for God, His way is perfect. PSALM 18:30

OCTOBER 4

Easter Sunday is the most triumphant and joyous day in the calendar of the Christian Church—and it should be!... The wonder of His resurrection is symbolized in the hope that beats in the hearts of believers everywhere as they sing triumphantly: "Christ the Lord is risen today." It is the message "Jesus is alive!" that lifts Christianity out of the category of dead superstitions and archaic religions and makes it the abiding faith of millions.... And now God's promise is for you: "If you confess with your mouth the Lord Jesus and believe in your heart that God has raised Him from the dead, you will be saved" (Romans 10:9).

MARCH 27

Almost anything can become an "idol"—something we worship and serve in place of God. It might be success, or pleasure, or possessions, or money, or anything else we let control our lives.… We substitute them for God—and as a result, we turn our backs on Him and never come to know Him and love Him as we should. Has any "idol" taken God's rightful place in your life? Don't let it happen. God has commanded, "You shall have no other gods before Me" (Exodus 20:3).

OCTOBER 5

The chairman of the history department of one of our great universities once stated his opinion to me, "We have become a nation of cowards." I challenged his statement, but he argued that many people have become reluctant to follow a course if it isn't popular. I had to admit he was right.... How different from the early Christians!... They boldly proclaimed the Gospel in the face of hostility, persecution, scorn, and even death.... You may never face the same dangers those early Christians did, but don't take the road of cowardice; don't give in to fear. Remember: "If God is for us, who can be against us?" (Romans 8:31).

MARCH 26

Aliens from other countries are rarely shown the "welcome mat."... They may even find themselves victims of discrimination, rejection, or intolerance. The Bible says that we are "aliens and strangers in the world" (1 Peter 2:11 NIV).... Our customs are different, our goals are different, our ways of living are different, our concerns are different. And as Christ's followers...we may find ourselves scorned, rejected, or even persecuted. If so, we shouldn't be surprised. Jesus warned, "If they persecuted Me, they will also persecute you" (John 15:20). But never forget: You are a citizen of the Kingdom of God. And some day you will be Home!

OCTOBER 6

The answer to our individual fears is found in a personal faith in the living, glorified Lord. And the answer to collective fear is a corporate faith in the living, glorified Lord. The answer to national and international tensions and fears is for the world to know Him who is alive forevermore.

Do not be afraid. MATTHEW 28:10

MARCH 25

Of Eric Liddell, the missionary and great runner whose story is told in the film *Chariots of Fire*, someone has said, he was "ridiculously humble in victory, utterly generous in defeat." That's a good definition of what it means to be meek.... Meekness involves being yielded.... Those who submit to the will of God do not fight back at life. They learn the secret of yielding—of relinquishing and abandoning—their own lives and wills to Christ. And then He gives back to them a life that is far richer and fuller than anything they could ever have imagined.

OCTOBER 7

Months after September 11, 2001, terrorist attacks on New York and Washington, psychiatrists reported that people who lived thousands of miles away from those tragic events were still coming to them, unable to sleep and paralyzed by fear…. What is the answer to stifling fear? After Jesus had been put to death His disciples huddled in fear behind closed doors, filled with uncertainty and despair. But suddenly they found themselves in the presence of their living Lord, and at His first words their fear disappeared: "Peace to you" (Luke 24:36)…. We worship a risen Christ, who has broken the power of sin and death and Hell and is alive forevermore. Why then should we fear?

MARCH 24

Having an attitude of thankfulness is all of life's circumstances will help you react as old Matthew Henry did when he was mugged. He wrote in his diary, "Let me be thankful first because I was never robbed before; second, although they took my purse, they did not take my life; third, because although they took my all, it was not much; and fourth, because it was I who was robbed, not I who robbed." I wonder if I could be that thankful!

OCTOBER 8

There are two ways of getting out of a trial. One is to simply try to get rid of the trial, and be thankful when it is over. The other is to recognize the trial as a challenge from God to claim a larger blessing than we have ever had…. As Peter Marshall once put it, "God will not permit any troubles to come upon us, unless He has a specific plan by which great blessing can come out of the difficulty."

Through God we will do valiantly.
PSALM 108:13

MARCH 23

Just as Jesus triumphed over death, so He helps us triumph over trouble. Even in the midst of troubles, the Bible says, "I will turn their mourning to joy" (Jeremiah 31:13).

How does it happen? By looking in faith to God. He has not abandoned us, and He has plans for our future. He can even give us an optimistic spirit—somewhat like the Englishman I heard about during World War II who stood looking at the deep hole in the ground where his bombed-out home had once stood. "I always did want a basement, I did," he said. "Now I can jolly well build another house like I always wanted!"

OCTOBER 9

We have not yet learned that a man can be more powerful on his knees than behind the most powerful weapons ever developed. We have not learned that a nation is more powerful when it unites in earnest prayer to God than when its resources are channeled into weapons.... Our basic problems are spiritual in nature, and only spiritual solutions will solve them. That is why prayer is so vital, for only God can change the human heart.

Who knows what might happen if millions of believers around the world availed themselves of the greatest privilege this side of heaven—the privilege of intercessory prayer? Will you be one of them?

MARCH 22

Perhaps…you are passing through a wilderness right now. It may be the wilderness of a broken marriage, or a financial reversal, or a major disappointment, or a threatening illness. It may even be a wilderness of doubt or sin. But God is with you in the wilderness, and He goes before you to encourage and guide you. He brought the children of Israel through the wilderness—and He will bring you through it as well, as you look in faith to Him. Never forget: "He is the living God, and steadfast forever" (Daniel 6:26).

OCTOBER 10

Jesus wept tears of compassion at the graveside of a friend. He mourned over Jerusalem because its people had lost their sensitivity to God and His Word. His great heart was always sensitive to the needs of others.... Jesus' love was more than human compassion, however; it was in the fullest sense divine love, for He was God in human flesh. This is the kind of love He calls us to have—and the kind He will give us as we seek it from Him.

Love the Lord your God with all your heart...
and your neighbor as yourself. LUKE 10:27

MARCH 21

The word redeem means to "buy back"—to recover by paying a price. The word redeemed can be illustrated from the ancient world by the position of a slave who had been captured in battle or enticed into serving one who was not his legal master. His real master, however, intent on recovering his slave's service and love, would buy him back—redeem him from the enemy— at great personal cost. That is what God did for us…. By His death on the Cross, Jesus paid the price for our deliverance, a price far greater than our true value. He did it solely because He loved us. Now we have been redeemed!

OCTOBER 11

The moment you come to Christ, the Spirit of God brings the life of God into you and you begin to live…. There's a whole new direction to your life, because now the Spirit of God has implanted within you the very life of God, Himself, who is eternal. And that means you will live as long as God lives! Too many Christians let themselves get bogged down by the cares and routines of daily living. Don't let that happen to you. Ask God to help you live each day with eternity in view.

MARCH 20

A disciple in Jesus' time was someone who followed a teacher or philosopher. A disciple was both a learner and a follower—believing the teacher's message and then putting it into practice. Jesus gave the word disciple added meaning, however, because His disciples also went out to tell others about Him. A disciple of Jesus, therefore, is someone who has committed his or her life to Jesus, and seeks each day to learn, to follow, and to share Him with others. Does this describe you?

If you abide in My word, you are My disciples indeed. JOHN 8:31

OCTOBER 12

One day an ugly caterpillar climbs into a tree and spins a silky robe about itself. It goes to sleep, and in a few weeks emerges a beautiful butterfly. So we—discouraged, unhappy, hounded by guilt, confused, depressed, vainly looking for an escape—can come by faith to Christ and emerge a new person. We can be born again! It sounds incredible, even impossible—and yet it is precisely what happens.... Do you feel you are in a cocoon? Turn to Christ and ask Him to give you your beautiful wings so that you might soar above your problems and be victorious over them.

MARCH 19

From time to time I have had people pour out their heart to me because their sins had been discovered…. They wept bitterly because they had devastated their marriage or ruined their reputation. But later…they were back in the same situation…. What was the problem? The problem was lack of repentance. Their tears were tears of self-pity—but not of repentance. True repentance is a turning from sin—a conscious, deliberate decision to leave sin behind—and a conscious turning to God, with a commitment to follow His will…. The Bible says, "Godly sorrow brings repentance that leads to salvation and leaves no regret" (2 Corinthians 7:10 NIV).

OCTOBER 13

The Bible does not condemn money or material possessions. Money and possessions can do great good, when they are used wisely and kept in proper perspective. Some of the great people of the Bible were very rich. Abraham, Isaac, and Solomon were perhaps the richest men of their day. God's quarrel is not with material goods but with material gods. Materialism has become the god of too many of us.... Don't let money, or anything else, take God's rightful place in your life.

What will it profit a man if he gains the whole world, and loses his own soul? MARK 8:36

MARCH 18

There are two ways to respond to adversity: discouragement and trust. The problem with giving in to discouragement is that it only makes things worse, for with it may come bitterness, anger, jealousy, revenge, and so forth.... One of the best ways to overcome adversity, I've found, is to praise God right in the middle of the turmoil. Turning to God's Word will also encourage us; many of the Psalms, for example, were written in the midst of suffering and adversity. Follow the Psalmist's example: "Bless the Lord, O my soul, and forget not all His benefits" (Psalm 103:2).

OCTOBER 14

I've been told that the French translation of this phrase, "Cast all your care upon Him" is "Unload your distress upon God." Have you ever seen a dump truck get rid of its load? The driver simply pushes a button or pulls on a lever and the heavy load is discharged at the prescribed spot.... We were never meant to be crushed under the weight of care.... Unload the anxieties of the present moment upon Him, for He cares for you. If He loved you enough to take away the burden of your sins, can't you trust Him to take away every lesser burden as well?

MARCH 17

I once saw a toy clown with a weight in its head.... It could be placed on its feet or on its side and when let go it flipped back on its head. The clown illustrates why the disciples seemed to be misfits in the world. To an upside-down man, a right-side-up man seems upside down. To the nonbeliever, the true Christian is an oddity and an abnormality. Yet this isn't the whole picture, for all around us are people who sense something is wrong with their topsy-turvy lives, and they yearn to be right side up. Will you pray for them and ask God to help you point them to life's only solid foundation—Jesus Christ?

OCTOBER 15

Once when we were on a flight from Korea to Japan, we flew through a rough snowstorm...so the pilot had to make an instrument landing. I sat up in the cockpit with him and watched him sweat it out as the watchful men in the airport tower guided him in. I did not want these men to be broad-minded.... I knew that our lives depended on their precise instructions. Just so, when we come in for the landing in the great airport of heaven, I don't want any broad-minded advice.... I want to be sure of a safe landing there. And I am sure, because Christ has gone before me and has provided the way.

MARCH 16

A missionary in China who was imprisoned by the Japanese during World War II, managed to take a forbidden Gospel of John with her into prison. She carefully hid it, and each night when she went to bed, she pulled the covers over her head and memorized one verse.... When the prisoners were released... the missionary was so chipper someone said she must have been brainwashed. A *Life* magazine reporter who had interviewed her said, "She's been brainwashed for sure. God washed her brain."... The Psalmist declared, "Your word I have hidden in my heart, that I might not sin against You" (Psalm 119:11).... Is God's Word stored up in your heart and mind for the future?

OCTOBER 16

When Jesus Christ is the source of our joy, no words can describe it. It is a joy "inexpressible and glorious" (1 Peter 1:8 NIV). Christ is the answer to the sadness and discouragement, the discord and division in our world. He can take discouragement and despondence out of our lives and replace them with optimism and hope…. When our confidence is in Him, discouragement gets crowded out. May that be true in your life today!

My soul shall be joyful in the Lord.
PSALM 35:9

MARCH 15

There are three elements to a successful marriage. The first is love—not just an emotional feeling or a physical attraction, but a deep commitment to put the other person first…. Maturity is the second ingredient in a successful marriage…. Maturity means a willingness to act responsibly and not take the easy way out. Third, faith must be an ingredient for a marriage to be successful. Marriage is difficult enough these days with all of life's pressures, but without Christ at the center of a marriage and a home, it becomes even more difficult…. I have seldom seen a marriage fail with the husband and wife pray and worship God together.

He who loves his wife loves himself.
EPHESIANS 5:28

OCTOBER 17

You cannot stop a baby's cry by giving him a rattle when he is hungry. He will keep on crying until his hunger is satisfied by the food his little body demands. Neither can the soul of a mature person be satisfied apart from God. David described the hunger of every human being when he said: "As the deer pants for the water brooks, so pants my soul for You, O God" (Psalm 42:1).

MARCH 14

"Come near to God and he will come near to you" (James 4:8 NIV). What a blessed promise and provision this is! It means each of us can come close to God, with the assurance He will come close to us—so close that we become conscious of His presence.... Whatever it takes, make time to be alone with God. Remember: He wants your fellowship, and He has done everything possible to make it a reality. He has forgiven your sins, at the cost of His own dear Son. He has given you His Word, and the priceless privilege of prayer and worship. He will come near to you, if you will come near to Him.

OCTOBER 18

A bar of raw steel may be purchased for a few dollars. But when that bar of steel has been thrust into the fires and processed, when it has been tempered and forged and made into tiny watch springs for expensive watches, it is worth thousands of dollars.... God through the refining fire of His Spirit performs a thousand miracles a day in the spiritual realm. His regenerating power can take the dull and ordinary things of our lives—even the burned-out ashes of our past—and forge them into something useful, even beautiful, for His purposes.

MARCH 13

The Holy Spirit helps us in life's struggles, and we must never forget that. But the Holy Spirit also plays two other important roles we must not overlook. First, He convicts us of sin. The Bible says, "He will convict the world of sin, and of righteousness, and of judgment" (John 16:8). While this verse focuses on His convicting power among unbelievers, the Holy Spirit also convicts believers when we sin. The second role of the Holy Spirit is as Teacher…. Just as surely as the Holy Spirit inspired the writers of the Bible, so He will instruct us as we meditate on God's Word. Are you a willing student of the Holy Spirit?

OCTOBER 19

Many intellectuals are asking where history is going. Will society get better and better—or will we end up destroying ourselves?… The last chapter of history will not be written by any human leader, however good or bad. Only God will write it. And write it He will.

Some day, when the human race stands at the edge of the abyss of self-destruction, God will intervene. It may be tomorrow, it may be a thousand years from now. But the outcome is certain—the future belongs to the Kingdom of God. Never forget: If you belong to the King, you are on the winning side!

Your throne, O God, is forever and ever.
PSALM 45:6

MARCH 12

The word compassion comes from two Latin words meaning "to suffer with." What better picture to describe God's compassion for us?... The greatest act of compassion in the history of the human race was the Cross, for there Christ suffered for us. He endured sin's penalty so we would not have to endure it ourselves. Now He calls us to have compassion on others, for His sake—to suffer with them, and to point them to the One who suffered for them. The Bible says, "Be sympathetic, love as brothers, be compassionate and humble" (1 Peter 3:8 NIV).

OCTOBER 20

Children are not bashful about asking for things. They would not be normal if they did not boldly make their needs known. God has said to His children, "Let us...come boldly to the throne of grace, that we may obtain mercy and find grace to help in time of need" (Hebrews 4:16). God is keenly aware that we are dependent upon Him for life's necessities. It was for that reason that Jesus said, "Ask, and it will be given to you; seek, and you will find; knock, and it will be opened to you" (Matthew 7:7).

MARCH 11

The first disciples weren't perfect, and neither are we. Like them, we need to learn more and follow more, and share more. But all of us who belong to Christ are called to be disciples. Unlike the original disciples, we can't physically spend time with Jesus, but we can learn from Him by reading His Word. We can follow Him by obeying His will. And we can share Him with a world that desperately needs to be saved.

OCTOBER 21

A refuge is a place safely out of harm's way. A fortress is a fortified building that is virtually impenetrable by conventional means. Martin Luther wrote a wonderful hymn that says, "A mighty fortress is our God; a bulwark never failing. Our helper He amidst the flood; of mortal ills prevailing." What a statement about the magnificent power and protection of God! Does God care for you and me? Can we turn to Him in trust and faith when troubles and temptations threaten to overwhelm us? Yes—a thousand times yes! What greater proof do we need than that He sent His Son, Jesus Christ, to die in our place?

He is my refuge and my fortress. PSALM 91:2

MARCH 10

Many people have difficulty believing God is a God of love.... If you really want to know the reality of God's love, look at the Cross.... It was love that restrained Him when He was falsely accused of blasphemy and led to Golgotha to die with common thieves. He raised not a hand against His enemies. It was love that kept Him from calling legions of angels to come to His defense. It was love that made Him, in a moment of agonizing pain, pause and give hope to a repentant sinner who cried, "Lord, remember me when You come into Your kingdom" (Luke 23:42).... Does God love us? Yes—and the proof is the Cross.

OCTOBER 22

Jesus had the most all-encompassing mind this world has ever seen. His convictions were so strong, so unswerving that He was not afraid to mingle with any group, secure in the knowledge that He would not be contaminated or swayed. Fear makes us unwilling to give voice to our convictions or to listen to those of others—fear of rejection, fear of our beliefs will be attacked, fear our faith might be shaken.... Never lose your confidence in the truth of the Gospel! But—like Jesus—may you always be "speaking the truth in love" (Ephesians 4:15).

MARCH 9

The human conscience is defiled by sin, says the Bible—and that is one reason it is not a reliable guide by itself. Our conscience needs to be cleansed by the purifying work of the Holy Spirit, and honed and sharpened by the truth of the Word of God. Satan can even twist our consciences if they are not yielded to Christ and convince us that wrong is really right. But in spite of its frailty, our conscience is still important, and God still uses it to warn us of danger.... Is God speaking to you about something that is not right in your life?... Face it, confess it, put it right, and never touch it again.

OCTOBER 23

Learn to trust God with a child-like dependence on Him as your loving heavenly Father and no trouble can destroy you. In those darkest hours before the Cross Jesus could still say, "I am not alone, because the Father is with Me" (John 16:32). The same is true for you. Even in that last dark hour of death, when your flesh and your heart fail, you will be able to depend in peace upon Him who "is the strength of my heart and my portion forever."

My flesh and my heart fail; but God is the strength of my heart. Psalm 73:26

MARCH 8

Dwight L. Moody was fond of pointing out that there are three kinds of faith in Jesus Christ: struggling faith, which is like a man floundering and fearful in deep water; clinging faith, which is like a man hanging to the side of a boat; and resting faith, which finds a man safe inside the boat—strong and secure enough to reach out his hand to help someone else.... Only one had discovered he could actually be in the boat—where all he had to do was rest. This is the kind of faith God wants us to have—a faith that trusts Him totally.

Come to Me...and I will give you rest.
MATTHEW 11:28

OCTOBER 24

I was reared during the Depression on a farm in North Carolina. My parents weren't able to give me the advantages most young people enjoy today. I grew up in a Christian home, but by the time I was fifteen, I was in full revolt against all religion—against God, the Bible, the church. But one night I committed my life to Jesus Christ, and He gave me a whole new direction.... No, I didn't become perfect, but my life was changed. I have been all over the world, and I have never met anyone who regretted giving his or her life to Christ. And neither will you.

MARCH 7

If you love someone, will you want to make him miserable? Will you go out of your way to punish him if he doesn't do exactly what you tell him to? No, of course not—not if you really love him. The same is true with God. God loves you, and because He loves you, He cares what happens to you. He loves you too much to let you wander aimlessly through life, without meaning or purpose. The Bible says, "You will show me the path of life; in Your presence is fullness of joy" (Psalm 16:11). Covet God's will for your life more than anything else. To know God's will— and to do it—is life's greatest joy.

OCTOBER 25

"Give," Christ commanded. Yet it was more than a command. It was an invitation to glorious and abundant living. If a person gets his attitude toward money right, it will help straighten out almost every other area of his life…. The chief motive of the selfish, unregenerate person is "get." The chief motive of the dedicated Christian should be "give." Jesus said, "Give, and it will be given to you." It's a promise, and we know Jesus never breaks His promises. Getting…or giving? Which is true of you?

Give, and it will be given to you. LUKE 6:38

MARCH 6

In the midst of a thousand different voices, all claiming their own authority and clamoring for our allegiance, only one Voice will tell us the truth. That Voice? The written Word of God, given to us by God to tell us what we are to believe and how we are to live. As the Psalmist said, "The entrance of Your words gives light" (Psalm 119:130)….

Coleridge said he believed the Bible to be the Word of God because… "It finds me."

"If you want encouragement," John Bunyan wrote, "entertain the promises."

Martin Luther said, "In Scriptures, even the little daisy becomes a meadow." The Bible is our one sure guide in an unsure world.

OCTOBER 26

During His lifetime on earth, Christ's presence could be experienced only by a small group of people at any given time. Now Christ dwells through the Spirit in the hearts of all who have received Him as Savior and Lord. The apostle Paul wrote, "Do you not know...that the Spirit of God dwells in you?" (1 Corinthians 3:16).... The Holy Spirit is given to every believer—not for a limited time, but forever. If He left us for one moment, we would be in deep trouble. But He doesn't! You will never have more of the Holy Spirit than you do right now. But will He have more of you?

MARCH 5

The Bible warned the people of Noah's day, "My Spirit shall not strive with man forever" (Genesis 6:3).... Eventually God's patience gave out—and by then it was too late. Outside the ark men and women struggled for their lives, clutching at pieces of driftwood, until the pitiless hand of death reached up and drew them down beneath those cruel waves. All were lost. Every soul outside the ark perished. They had had their chance, but tossed it away.... Come to Christ while there is still time. Christ, God's greater Ark, stands ready to welcome you to safety today. Are you in the Ark?

OCTOBER 27

George Sweeting has said, "Life minus love equals nothing!" Do you have this kind of love—a love that puts others ahead of yourself? Without Jesus Christ in your heart, without the Holy Spirit in your life, you can't produce this love…. This is one reason we must receive Christ, for apart from His Spirit we can never be freed from the chains of selfishness, jealousy, and indifference. Will others see Christ's love in your life today?

All the law is fulfilled in one word;…love your neighbor as yourself. GALATIANS 5:14

MARCH 4

In the face of chastening, adversity, discipline, and affliction, God's Word nourishes our lives and fruit begins to appear. But it doesn't happen overnight.... Joseph would never have been of use to God had he not been sold into slavery by brothers who hated him, and then wrongly accused by Potiphar, who put him in prison. Even after he had told Pharaoh's cupbearer he would be restored to the king's court and asked him to tell Pharaoh of his unjust imprisonment, Joseph had to wait two more years for release from prison. As we wait upon the Lord, He may sometimes seem slow in coming to help us, but He never comes too late. His timing is always perfect.

OCTOBER 28

Jesus used the carefree attitude of the birds to underscore the fact that worrying is unnatural. "Look at the birds of the air, for they neither sow nor reap;...yet your heavenly Father feeds them" (Matthew 6:26). If He cares for tiny birds and frail flowers, why can't we count on Him for every aspect of our lives? After all, He loves us so much that He sent His Son into the world to save us. We are that valuable to Him!

MARCH 3

Some day we who know Christ will have perfect bodies—bodies that will never age or experience pain. Some day our dead bodies will be "raised in glory" (1 Corinthians 15:43), and we will be like Christ in His resurrection body. Can I imagine what that will be like? Not fully. But I do know this: The resurrected body of Jesus is the pattern or design for our new bodies. "For our citizenship is in heaven, from which we eagerly wait for the Savior, the Lord Jesus Christ, who will transform our lowly body that it may be conformed to His glorious body" (Philippians 3:20-21). What a future we have in Christ!

OCTOBER 29

Christ instructed His followers to pray at all times, both by His teaching and His example. So fervent and so direct were His prayers that once, after He finished praying, His followers pleaded, "Lord, teach us to pray" (Luke 11:1). They yearned to be in touch with God, as they knew Christ was. Have you ever said, "Lord, teach me to pray?" Prayer shouldn't be casual or sporadic, dictated only by the needs of the moment. Prayer should be as much a part of our lives as breathing. Never has our world stood in greater need of people who will pray. Will you be one of them?

MARCH 2

When Satan tried to trap Jesus at the beginning of His ministry, he used the same temptations he uses today. One trap was the lure of things....

Isaiah said, "Listen carefully to Me...and let your soul delight itself in abundance" (Isaiah 55:2). Yes, delight in abundance—the abundance God gives you, both material and spiritual. Especially delight in the abundance of joy that comes from His presence. Satan will always offer you substitutes. Refuse them!

OCTOBER 30

The Gulf Stream flows in the ocean, and yet it is not absorbed by it. It maintains its warm temperatures even in the icy waters of the North Atlantic.... If Christians are to fulfill their purposes in the world, they must not be chilled by the indifferent, godless society in which they live. The Bible says, "Do not be conformed to this world" (Romans 12:2). It is true that Jesus dined with publicans and sinners, but He did not allow the social group to overwhelm Him and conform Him to its ways.... As you have contact with others this day, will they sense the warmth of Christ's presence through you?

MARCH 1

When the Standard Oil Company was looking for a representative in the Far East, they approached a missionary and offered him $10,000. He turned down the offer. They raised it to $25,000, and he turned it down again. They raised it to $50,000, and he rejected it once more. "What's wrong?" they asked. He replied, "Your price is all right, but your job is too small." God had called him to be a missionary, and anything else was not worthy of his consideration. What should we be for Jesus Christ?... Nothing less than God's call is worthy of our consideration.

OCTOBER 31

When I think about God's love I tend to dwell upon all the good things He has done for me. But then I must stop and realize that even when circumstances have been hard or the way unclear, God has still surrounded me with His love. God's love is just as real and just as powerful in the darkness as it is in the light. And that is why we can have hope!

Every day I turn to the Bible to give me strength and wisdom for the day and hope for the future.

FEBRUARY 29

Have you ever faced a situation that was so overwhelming or so confusing you didn't even know how to pray about it? Have you ever been so overcome with grief or burdened by heartache you couldn't put your emotions into words—much less pray about them?

What a comfort these words should be: "The Spirit helps us in our weakness. We do not know what we ought to pray, but the Spirit himself intercedes for us...in accordance with God's will" (Romans 8:26-27 NIV).... Turn to God in every situation—even when you don't feel like it. The Spirit is interceding for you, in accordance with God's will.

NOVEMBER 1

Popularity and praise can be far more dangerous for the Christian than persecution. They can turn us away from God without our even being aware of it, making us like those in Jesus' day who "loved the praise of men far more than the praise of God" (John 12:43).

Unfortunately, it is easy when all goes well to lose our perspective.... Ask God to keep you from worrying about what others think, and to be content with whatever He sends your way. All the tomorrows of our lives have to pass Him before they get to us!

FEBRUARY 28

Sometimes I almost wish Thomas Jefferson had not inserted those words in the American Declaration of Independence about "the pursuit of happiness." He was correct, of course; God has given us the "right" (or at least the freedom) to pursue happiness. The problem is that millions think this must be the primary purpose of life.... In the end, however, their search ends in disillusionment.... True happiness comes from a different pursuit—the pursuit of God. He has promised, "You will seek Me and find Me, when you search for Me with all your heart" (Jeremiah 29:13). That promise is true—because God also pursues us. He even sent His Son into the world to pursue us and bring us to heaven. Only God gives true happiness.

NOVEMBER 2

As much as our homes mean to us, they are not permanent.... Those disciples who, for Christ's sake, gave up houses and lands and loved ones, knew little of home life or home joys.... The venerable Bishop Ryle is reputed to have said, "Heaven is a prepared place for a prepared people, and those who enter shall find that they are neither unknown or unexpected." Even life's happiest experiences last but a moment, yet heaven's joy is eternal. Some days we will go to our eternal Home—and Christ will be there to welcome us!

FEBRUARY 27

The family is the most important institution in the world.... In the home, character and integrity are formed, values are made clear, and goals are set. These last a lifetime. And if they aren't formed correctly, that, too, will result in patterns—bad patterns—that last a lifetime, if God doesn't intervene. Today, Satan is attacking the family as never before. But what are our defenses against such attacks? As always, our best defense is the Word of God. Read the Bible together as a family. Have family devotions. Pray for one another daily by name.... And most of all, commit your marriage to Christ, and make Him the center of your home—and your life.

NOVEMBER 3

Think of the blessings we so easily take for granted: Life itself; preservation from danger; every bit of health we enjoy; every hour of liberty; the ability to see, to hear, to speak, to think, and to imagine—all this comes from the hand of God. Even our capacity to love is a gift from God. Most of all, God has given us the gift of Christ.... What have you done lately to show your gratitude to God for all that He has done, and is doing, for you?

I have learned in whatever state I am, to be content. PHILIPPIANS 4:11

FEBRUARY 26

We are not the masters of our fate. We think we control our lives—but we don't. In an instant life can radically change—a car accident, a heart attack, a pink slip, a child's raging fever. Frustrated researchers conquer one deadly virus, only to discover one even more lethal.... No book is more realistic about the human situation than the Bible. It won't let us get by with frothy platitudes or unsupported optimism. But it also gives us hope. It tells us Christ can change our lives, and He has prepared a perfect place for us in heaven. Even your next breath is a gift from God. Don't take life for granted, but "gain a heart of wisdom" (Psalm 90:12).

NOVEMBER 4

Simon Peter was so spiritually weak before Pentecost that, in spite of his bragging to the contrary, he swore and denied Christ. He was cowed by the crowd, shamed by a little maid, and took his place with the enemies of Christ. But see him after he has been baptized with fire—the fire of the Holy Spirit!… Peter, the weak, was transformed into Peter, the rock. So it was with the early disciples. The Holy Spirit changed them from ordinary individuals into firebrands for God…. Their secret? Total submission to Jesus Christ and His will. What keeps you from being used of God to touch your world for Christ?

FEBRUARY 25

Just as our bodies have certain characteristics and appetites, so do our souls.... The soul has an appetite for God—a yearning to be reconciled to its Creator and to have fellowship with Him forever. In our world, we give most of our attention to satisfying the appetites of the body and practically none to the soul. Consequently we are one-sided. We become fat physically and materially, while spiritually we are lean, weak, and anemic. The soul actually demands as much attention as the body. It demands fellowship and communion with God. It demands worship, quietness, and meditation. Nothing but God ever completely satisfies, because the soul was made for God. Don't starve your soul.

NOVEMBER 5

God does not bargain with us, nor can we barter with Him. He holds our eternal salvation in His omnipotent hand, and He bids us take it as a free gift, "without money and without price."... Salvation is free—but it wasn't cheap. It cost the dear Son of God His very life.

Only cheap, tawdry things have a price tag on them. The best things in life are free—the air we breathe, the stars at night, the wonder of human love. But the greatest gift of all is our salvation, purchased for us by Jesus Christ. "Thanks be to God for His indescribable gift!" (2 Corinthians 9:15).

FEBRUARY 24

What would you do if you met a lion? You'd probably run, and you'd probably grab any weapon you could to fend him off if he attacked. And that is true in our struggles against evil. When evil and temptation stalk us, our first response should be to flee. And when they still attack, we should use every weapon we have to drive them away. The good news is this: God has provided the weapons! His Word, His angels, His Spirit, the encouragement and prayers of our brothers and sisters in Christ—these and more are "weapons" God provides. We aren't in this battle alone—so why act like it?

NOVEMBER 6

We are holding a light.... Though it may seem but a twinkling candle in a world of blackness, it is our business to let it shine.

We are blowing a trumpet.... We must keep sounding the alarm to those who are in spiritual danger....

We are kindling a fire. In this cold world full of hatred and selfishness our little blaze may seem to be unavailing, but we must keep our fire burning.

A light, a trumpet, a fire...they seem so little.... But "with God all things are possible" (Matthew 19:26), and He will bless our efforts to bring the good news of Jesus to a weary and strife-torn world.

FEBRUARY 23

Some people think Christians should always be smiling and happy, and something is wrong if they aren't. But this isn't necessarily true. Jesus stood outside the tomb of His friend Lazarus, and we read that "Jesus wept" (John 11:35). As He approached Jerusalem "He saw the city and wept" (Luke 19:41) because of its spiritual blindness and guilt. He knelt in the Garden of Gethsemane and was "in agony...[and] His sweat became like great drops of blood" (Luke 22:44). Don't confuse happiness with joy.... Life's troubles will rob us of our happiness, but they can never rob us of the joy God gives us, as we turn in faith to Him and seek His face.

NOVEMBER 7

Two conflicting forces cannot exist in one human heart. When doubt reigns, faith cannot abide. Where hatred rules, love is crowded out. Where selfishness rules, there love cannot dwell. When worry is present, trust cannot crowd its way in. In the same way, God will not share His rightful place in our lives with anything or anyone less than Himself. Is anything crowding God out of your heart today? Don't give first place to anything less than Christ, but "commit your way to the Lord."

Commit your way to the Lord...and He shall bring it to pass. PSALM 37:5

FEBRUARY 22

The Old Testament gives a wonderful picture of God as our Shepherd.... In the best-known of all Psalms, David makes the relationship personal. "The Lord is my shepherd," he cries exultantly, "I shall lack nothing." He then tells of God's constant care, until that day when "I will dwell in the house of the Lord forever" (Psalm 23:6 NIV). But the New Testament tells of another Shepherd—the Lord Jesus Christ: "I am the good shepherd. The good shepherd gives His life for the sheep" (John 10:11). He guides and protects us, and even gave His life so we will be safely in His fold forever.

NOVEMBER 8

The Bible says, "Pray without ceasing." It isn't enough to get out of bed in the morning, quickly bow our head, and repeat a few sentences. Instead, we need to set aside specific times to be alone with God, speaking to Him in prayer and listening to Him speak through His Word.... For the overworked mother or other busy person this may seem impossible.... But even when we are busy, we can "pray without ceasing" in our hearts and minds. We can pray anywhere, any time—and God will hear us. Today let prayer saturate your life "without ceasing."

Rejoice always, pray without ceasing.
1 THESSALONIANS 5:16–17

FEBRUARY 21

You may be a worrier by nature, but even the worst worrier in the world doesn't worry about some things!... Ask yourself why you do not worry about such things. Is it because, in the case of running water, it has always been there when you wanted it?... Certainty breeds trust, doesn't it?... We can be just as certain and just as worry-free about God's love and protection. What is the evidence? It is the Cross, where God fully expressed His love for us.... His love is certain. He has never gone back on a single promise, and He never will.

The Lord is near to all who call upon Him, to all who call upon Him in truth. PSALM 145:18

NOVEMBER 9

Conscience has been described as the light of the soul. Even when it is dulled or darkened by sin, it can still bear witness to the reality of good and evil, and to the holiness of God. What causes this warning light to go on inside me when I do wrong? It is my conscience, given by God to steer me away from evil toward good.... Persistent sin can dull or even silence our conscience. On the other hand, persistent attention to God's Word will sharpen our conscience and make us more sensitive to moral or spiritual danger. Is this happening in your life?

FEBRUARY 20

Our spiritual problems can only be solved by the God who created us originally.... Today by the grace of His Son, He can re-create us in the likeness of His resurrection. Through faith in Jesus Christ, we are recreated and become partakers of His life. Just as we were born again by the Spirit of God, so we grow and become more like Christ as the Spirit works in our lives. "Therefore, if anyone is in Christ, he is a new creation; old things have passed away; behold, all things have become new" (2 Corinthians 5:17). Don't be chained to the past. You are a new creation in Christ!

NOVEMBER 10

God has a plan for peace, and it is found in His Son, whom the Bible calls the "Prince of Peace" (Isaiah 9:6). But we have rejected God's plan. Wars still ravage our world—and our lives. Why? Jesus said the problem is within us.... Our real war is a rebellion against God—and it brings unending misery. But God longs to see this rebellion cease.... This happens as we repent and receive Christ. The war is over, for God extends a peace treaty to all who come to Christ.

FEBRUARY 19

Some day we will go to a home where all is happiness, joy, and peace. How barren our lives would be if we didn't have this hope. Knowing heaven is real will make a difference in the way we live. For one thing, we won't become attached to the things of this world. We will say with Paul, "I have learned in whatever state I am, to be content" (Philippians 4:11). But heaven should also give us a burden for those who do not have this hope. Every day you meet people who do not know Christ. Will you tell them?

NOVEMBER 11

As God's children, we are His dependents. Dependent children spend little time worrying about meals, clothing, and shelter. They assume—and they have a right to—that their parents will provide everything they need. Jesus said, "Do not worry, saying, 'What shall we eat?' or 'What shall we drink?' or 'What shall we wear?'.... But seek first the kingdom of God...and all these things shall be added to you" (Matthew 6:31, 33).

FEBRUARY 18

From the very beginning, since man sinned against God, the family has been in trouble…. The reason the family is in critical condition today is that we have neglected His rules for a successful home. We have put self in place of sacrifice. We have valued things more than we have valued people. You can have the right kind of home. Your home can be united if it is now divided. The place to begin is on your knees, asking Christ for forgiveness and then asking God to give you a new love for each other—and for Him. Don't let your family drift apart, but with God's help resist the pressures and come together around the Cross.

NOVEMBER 12

"Daddy, how can I believe in the Holy Spirit when I have never seen Him?" asked Jim…. The father took Jim to a power plant and showed him the generators…. "We can't see the power, but it's in that machine and in the power lines," said the father….

"Do you believe in electricity?" he asked. "Yes, I believe in electricity," said Jim.

"Of course you do," said his father, "Likewise, you can believe in the Holy Spirit not because you see Him, but you see what He does in people's lives when they are surrendered to Christ and possess His power."

FEBRUARY 17

The late British historian, Arnold Toynbee, gave his personal slogan to the world when he said, "Cling, and hope." In other words, he says, all the ideals we held a few years ago are crumbling; but he advised the human race to cling and hope. But to what?... Multiplied thousands have found that faith in Christ is more than adequate for the pressures of this hour. The true Christian does more than "cling and hope." He knows that with Christ he is secure forever. Is your hope in Him?

The Lord will be a shelter for His people.
JOEL 3:16

NOVEMBER 13

Your life may seem monotonous and filled with drudgery. Yet remember, if you are a Christian, you are not working for an hour or for a day but for eternity. When this body of corruption shall take on immortality, another part of our work will begin, for the Scripture teaches that God's servants shall serve Him forever. The difference is that in heaven we will never grow bored or weary!... Because Christ is alive, we have "an inheritance incorruptible and undefiled...reserved in heaven" (1 Peter 1:4). And this helps us persevere, even when life seems dull.

FEBRUARY 16

What proofs did Jesus offer that He was truly God come in human form? First, there was proof of His perfect life.... Second, there was evidence of His miraculous power.... Third, there was the evidence of fulfilled prophecy.... Fourth, there was the evidence of His resurrection from the dead. Fifth, there is the proof of changed lives.

Christ alone, the divine Son of God, has power to change the human heart. And He does.... Faith in Christ is not a "leap in the dark." It is based on the solid facts of Christ's life, death and resurrection. Thank God that we have a solid foundation in Him!

NOVEMBER 14

The early Christians had no buildings, no airplanes, no automobiles, no printing presses or television or radio. Yet they…started a spiritual revolution that shook the very foundations of the Roman Empire. In the face of opposition and overwhelming odds they stayed courageous, bold, dauntless, and full of faith…. What was their secret? The Bible gives us the key: "They were all filled with the Holy Spirit" (Acts 2:4). The Holy Spirit changed their lives, and those they met couldn't help but be impressed by their love and the quality and purity of their lives. What keeps us from turning our world "upside down" for Christ?

FEBRUARY 15

What would you say about a person who had made a hundred promises to you and already kept ninety-nine of them? You probably would think he was honest enough to fulfill the last promise as well, wouldn't you? Jesus Christ has fulfilled every promise He ever made, except one. He has not yet returned. Will He? In both the Old and New Testaments there are references to the return of the Lord.... The entire book of Revelation tells of the glorious return of Christ. And we can say with the apostle John, who wrote that book, "Amen. Even so, come, Lord Jesus" (Revelation 22:20).... Are you seeking until that day to be His faithful servant?

NOVEMBER 15

How we live at home is the acid test for any Christian man or woman....

If I am a true Christian, I will not give way at home to bad temper, impatience, faultfinding, sarcasm, unkindness, suspicion, selfishness, or laziness. Instead, each day my life will display the fruit of the Spirit, which is "love, joy, peace, patience, kindness, goodness, faithfulness, gentleness, and self-control" (Galatians 5:22–23 NIV). How different would your home be if you consistently practiced these Christ-like virtues?

I am the vine, you are the branches. He who abides in Me, and I in him, bears much fruit.
JOHN 15:5

FEBRUARY 14

When English patriot Sir William Russell went to the scaffold in 1683, he took his watch out of his pocket and handed it to the physician who attended him in his death. "Would you kindly take my timepiece?" he asked. "I have no use for it. I am now dealing with eternity." This world fades into insignificance in the light of eternity. All the things that preoccupy us are no longer important, and only one thing counts: our relationship with God…. How different would today be if you knew it would be your last one on earth before meeting God face to face?

I will see Your face in righteousness; I shall be satisfied when I awake in your likeness.
PSALM 17:15

NOVEMBER 16

The Christian life is a joyful life. Christianity was never meant to be something to make people miserable. The ministry of Jesus Christ was one of joy. The Bible teaches that a life of inward peace and outward victory is a Christian's birthright. "What a witness to the world Christians would be," wrote Amy Carmichael, "if only they were more evidently very happy people." Joy is one of the marks of a true believer. Will others see the joy of Christ in your life today?

Rejoice in the Lord always. PHILIPPIANS 4:4

FEBRUARY 13

C.S. Lewis once observed that this life is only "shadow lands" compared to the glory to come. Even life at its best is but a shadow of heaven.... We experience the joy of marriage, knowing it is the foretaste of an even greater joy: the heavenly marriage feast of the Lamb (Revelation 19:9). We enjoy the beauty of God's creation, knowing it is the foretaste of an even greater beauty: the glory of heaven (Revelation 21:23). Take delight in the good things God gives you. Don't be too preoccupied to "smell the roses"!... Every one of His good gifts should remind us of the glory to come!

NOVEMBER 17

Nowhere does the Bible teach that Christians are exempt from tribulation and natural disaster.... But the Bible does teach that we can face trials with a power others do not have—the power of God. As we trust Him, God helps us endure, and even discern His purposes in the midst of suffering.... The eagle has the unique ability to lock its joints and soar effortlessly on an updraft, instead of flapping its wings. As we wait upon God, He helps us use the winds of adversity to soar above our problems. As the Bible says, "Those who wait on the Lord...shall mount up with wings like eagles" (Isaiah 40:31).

FEBRUARY 12

By any measure drug and alcohol dependence has become one of our greatest social problems.... I'm not a doctor, of course, and I fully realize some drugs have a legitimate place under careful medical supervision. But in my experience far too many people turn first to drugs or alcohol instead of to God. Rather than face their problems and deal with them (with God's help), they use drugs or alcohol to escape.... Don't let anything substitute for God. He loves you, and He wants to give you peace—the peace that comes from knowing Him. Jesus' promise to His followers is true: "I will give you rest" (Matthew 11:28).

I will...lie down in peace...for you alone...
make me dwell in safety. PSALM 4:8

NOVEMBER 18

Christ's first appearing was quiet, almost unnoticed—a humble manger, simple shepherds, an insignificant corner of the Roman Empire. His second appearing will be glorious and universal. He will be accompanied by His angels and will defeat every enemy until He subdues the whole earth. How easily the events of the moment crowd out the promise of eternity! The present seems so real; the unseen future seems so illusory. But in reality the opposite is true. Don't let the present consume you. Instead, "seek those things which are above, where Christ is" (Colossians 3:1).

FEBRUARY 11

All the masterpieces of painting contain both light and shadow.... A happy life is not one filled only with sunshine, but one that uses both light and shadow to produce beauty. Suffering or persecution can become a blessing because they can form a dark backdrop for the radiance of the Christian life.... Fanny Crosby, her spirit aglow with faith in Christ, saw more with her sightless eyes than most of us do with normal vision. She gave us some of the great gospel songs that cheer our hearts and lives.... Don't despise the shadows God brings into your life. He can use them to produce a masterpiece.

November 19

I knew a wealthy father who refused to get his son a bicycle because the boy's report card showed disgracefully low marks, the yard was not raked, and other assignments had not been carried out.... He wasn't being cruel or stingy; he simply knew his son needed to learn responsibility. God, too, wants us to learn responsibility. Yes, we are saved by His grace—but we are also called to be responsible disciples, learning to follow Christ by obeying God's will.... If you want God to hear your prayers, surrender your selfishness and stubbornness to Him, and then humbly seek His will. Obedience is the master key to effective prayer.

FEBRUARY 10

A young Irishman, Joseph Scriven (1820-1886), was deeply in love with a young woman, and their marriage plans had been made. The night before their wedding, however, she drowned in a tragic accident. For months Scriven was bitter, in utter despair. At last he turned to Christ, and through His grace, found peace and comfort. Out of this experience he wrote the familiar hymn that has brought consolation to millions...: "What a friend we have in Jesus / All our sins and griefs to bear!"...Even sorrows turn to blessings when they make us less attached to the earth and more attached to God. Then...we discover that Jesus truly is our friend—"All our sins and griefs to bear!"

NOVEMBER 20

We still wrestle with the same problems that preoccupied Plato and Aristotle centuries ago: Where did we come from? Why are we here? Where are we going?... But the Cross boldly stands against the confusion of our world, a beacon of hope in the midst of darkness and doubt. In the Cross, Christ not only bridged the gap between God and us, but there we find the answers to life's deepest questions.... Never underestimate what Christ did for us through the Cross. By it our salvation was won, and by it our lives—and our world—can be transformed. What difference does the Cross make in your life?

FEBRUARY 9

Jesus only distributed the bread He had miraculously provided for the crowds after "he had given thanks" (Matthew 15:36 NIV). At the Last Supper with His disciples, before facing the horror of the Cross, Jesus "gave thanks" (Luke 22:17, 19). It's easy to be thankful when God blesses us with something good—swift recovery from an illness, for example, or an advancement at work. But the Bible says we should "give thanks in all circumstances, for this is God's will for [us] in Christ Jesus" (1 Thessalonians 5:18 NIV). Thankfulness drives away a sour or prideful spirit. Make it part of your prayers every day.

NOVEMBER 21

Once while crossing the North Atlantic in a ship, I looked out my porthole when I got up in the morning and saw one of the blackest clouds I had ever seen…. I ordered my breakfast sent to my room and spoke to the steward about the storm. He said, "Oh, we've already come through that storm. It's behind us." If we are believers in Jesus Christ, we have already come through the storm of judgment. It happened at the Cross. Don't be bound by your guilt or your fears any longer, but realize that sin's penalty has already been paid by Christ—completely and fully.

FEBRUARY 8

The Pilgrim Fathers who landed at Plymouth in America in 1620 knew nothing of the bountiful prosperity that so many people enjoy today. During that first long winter, seven times as many graves were made for the dead as homes were built for the living…. Yet their lives were marked by a spirit of constant thankfulness. On one occasion William Brewster, rising from a scanty Plymouth dinner of clams and water, gave thanks to God "for the abundance of the sea and the treasures hid in the sand."… Ask God to open your eyes to all the blessings He has bestowed on you, and to give you a fresh spirit of gratitude—not just at this season of the year, but always.

NOVEMBER 22

People may seek to quench the thirst of their souls in a hundred other ways, but we must keep crying out, "Ho! Everyone who thirsts, come to the waters" (Isaiah 55:1). Sometimes they can't come, and we have to carry it to them. We must persevere. We must never give up. Christ never gave up, but "became obedient to the point of death" (Philippians 2:8). All around you are people who hunger and thirst for God, although they may not even realize it. Will you point them to Christ, who alone can satisfy their deepest longings?

He who wins souls is wise. PROVERBS 11:30

FEBRUARY 7

The Bible teaches that God is absolutely holy and pure.... Christ cried from the Cross, "My God, My God, why have You forsaken Me?" (Mark 15:34). What a horrible moment, as the blackness of human sin—now laid upon Christ—caused the Father to turn away in disgust.... We should be grateful for every gift God gives us. But the greatest gift of all is the gift of His Son, who endured the penalty we deserved for our sin, so we could be reconciled to a holy God. Never take that gift for granted! "Thanks be to God for his indescribable gift!" (2 Corinthians 9:15).

NOVEMBER 23

Many times when I go to bed at night I think that before I awaken Christ may come. Sometimes when I get up and look at the dawn I think that perhaps this is the day He will return. But until that day, God is still working—and so should we. In a world filled with turmoil and hopelessness, we are to pray, and we are to do all we can to alleviate suffering and bring Christ's love to others. May Jesus' words become true in your life: "Let your light shine before men, that they may see your good works and glorify your Father in heaven" (Matthew 5:16).

FEBRUARY 6

Separated from friends, unjustly accused, brutally treated—if any man had a right to complain it was this man, languishing almost forgotten in a harsh Roman prison. But instead of complaints, his lips rang with words of praise and thanksgiving! This was the apostle Paul…. Look carefully at what he wrote during that prison experience: "Sing and make music in your heart to the Lord, always giving thanks to God the Father for everything, in the name of our Lord Jesus Christ (Ephesians 5:19-20 NIV)…. Thanksgiving for Paul was not a once-a-year celebration, but a daily reality that made him a joyful person in every situation. May that be true of us.

November 24

Have you ever been under water for a period of time that is longer than you had expected? You know, as the time ticks away, how desperate you to become to reach the surface and breathe the air.... You have no other thoughts but quenching your need for air. That is what it means to "long for God," to feel unfulfilled without Him. It means we know we desperately need Him, even more than we need air, and we yearn to be filled with His presence.... Ask God to give you a new hunger for Him, so you may become filled with "the fullness of Christ" (Ephesians 4:13).

FEBRUARY 5

From Genesis to Revelation, from earth's greatest tragedy to earth's greatest triumph, the dramatic story of humanity's lowest depths and God's highest heights can be couched in twenty-five beautiful words: "For God so loved the world that He gave His only begotten Son, that whoever believes in Him should not perish but have everlasting life" (John 3:16).... God's holiness demands that all sin be punished, but God's love provided a plan of redemption and salvation for a lost and sinful world. By that plan Jesus Christ came from heaven to give His life as the final and perfect sacrifice for sin.... Have you put your faith in Him? If so, everlasting life is yours!

NOVEMBER 25

The word love is used to mean many different things. We say that we "love" the house that we have just bought or that we "love" a particular vacation spot or that we "love" a peanut butter and jelly sandwich. We also "love"…our husband or wife. Hopefully we don't love our spouse the same way we love a peanut butter and jelly sandwich!

The greatest love of all, however, is God's love for us—a love that showed itself in action…. How will you respond to His love today?

He loved us and sent His Son to be the propitiation for our sins. 1 JOHN 4:10

FEBRUARY 4

Today there is more knowledge in the world than ever before. Computers of fiber optic cables can transmit information in a millisecond to any part of the globe.... Yet that same century also recorded the most devastating wars and the fiercest genocides in human history. We have never been farther from solving our basic problems. The Bible says there are two kinds of wisdom in the world. First, there is wisdom that is given by God, a wisdom that views life in terms of eternity.... The second is the "wisdom of the world." This wisdom excludes God and His moral standards from human decisions.... But where has it gotten us? Which kind of wisdom will you choose?

NOVEMBER 26

My home is on a mountain nearly four thousand feet high.... Many times I have sat on our rustic front porch and watched the clouds below. I have thought of the clouds of discouragement and suffering that temporarily veil the sunlight of God's love from us. Many people live with a cloud hanging over their lives.

The Bible has a great deal to say about clouds, for they sometimes symbolize the spiritual forces that obscure the face of God. But He has not abandoned us. He is still there, and in faith we know we can trust His promise: "I will never leave you nor forsake you" (Hebrews 13:5).

FEBRUARY 3

Preparing for heaven is much like going on a journey. First, you must decide you want to go there. Next, you must purchase your ticket…. Can you buy it by being a good person? or going to church or acting religious?… the Bible says none of these will suffice, because the ticket to heaven is expensive—far too expensive for any human being to afford. Does that mean we can never go there? No—and the reason is because Someone else had already purchased the ticket for us. That person was Jesus Christ, and this price He paid was His own blood, shed on the Cross for us. Now He offers us the ticket to heaven free and fully paid! Why refuse it?

NOVEMBER 27

Jesus wants to be part of every experience and every moment of our lives.

He went to the wedding at Cana as well as to the home of Mary and Martha when Lazarus died. He wept with those who wept and rejoiced with those who rejoiced. Someone has said, "There are just as many stars in the sky at noon as at midnight, although we cannot see them with the sun's glare."... God is with us in the good times also, and we should thank Him for them and commit them to Him just as surely as we do the hard times.

FEBRUARY 2

At least two things happen when we give. First, when we give with the right attitude, God reminds us that what we have isn't really ours. He gave us everything we have, and it actually belongs to Him. King David prayed, "All things come from You, and of Your own we have given You" (1 Chronicles 29:14).... Second, when we give, we help meet the needs of others whom God also loves. By giving to others we testify to God's love for them, and we point them to the greatest gift of all—God's gift of His Son for our salvation.... God wants us to be channels of blessing to others. Are you?

NOVEMBER 28

C.T. Studd, the famous Cambridge cricketer and missionary pioneer, wrote the following couplet while still a student at Cambridge:

Only one life, 'twill soon be past;

Only what's done for Christ will last.

Life is a glorious opportunity if it is used to condition us for eternity.

If we fail in this, though we succeed in everything else, our life will have been a failure.... How will you spend it—for yourself, or for Christ? Remember: "Only what's done for Christ will last."

May the glory of the Lord endure forever; may the Lord rejoice in His works. PSALM 104:31

FEBRUARY 1

I may travel all over the world, but I know that when I come home, I will return to a precise location. It will still be there at the end of my journey, and I always look forward to coming home! In saying that He was going to prepare a place for us, Jesus was telling us that when we die, we are going to a precise location.... He said, "In my Father's house are many mansions" (John 14:2).... When we as Christians die, we go straight into the presence of Christ—straight to that place, straight to that mansion in heaven to spend eternity with God. We are simply changing our address!

NOVEMBER 29

The Bible teaches that our minds are to be brought under the control of Christ. The reason? How we act will be determined by how we think. If God is to change our lives, He must first change our minds. The human mind cannot be a vacuum. It will be filled either with good or evil. It will be filled either with Christ or with carnality. What will make the difference? It depends on us, and on what we allow to enter our minds....

Deliberately turn away from every evil thought today and ask God to fill your mind instead with Himself from this moment on.

JANUARY 31

God's Word never changes. Jesus said, "I tell you the truth, until heaven and earth disappear, not the smallest letter, not the least stroke of a pen, will by any means disappear from the Law" (Matthew 5:18 NIV).... This isn't because God is an inflexible or insensitive tyrant. It is because He knows what is best for us. He knows how we function, and He knows the pitfalls and dangers we face. If He didn't love us, He wouldn't try to guide us in the right path. But He does!... Let God's Word shape and guide you. God loves you too much to leave you in the dark!

You are my hiding place...; I hope in Your word. PSALM 119:114

NOVEMBER 30

In the Bible we are called "children of light and children of the day" (1 Thessalonians 5:5 NRSV), because it pleased God to share His mysteries and secrets with us. We are no longer in the dark—we know where we came from, we know why we are here, and we know where we are going. In the midst of the world living in spiritual darkness, walk as a child of the light!

You, brethren, are not in darkness…. You are all sons of light. 1 THESSALONIANS 5:4–5

JANUARY 30

When I imagine Christ hanging from the Cross, the spikes in His hands, the crown of thorns on His brow, His blood draining from His body, the soldiers mocking Him—then I begin to see the depth of God's grace. Then I know that nothing can equal the infinite love of God for a sinful world. But God's grace is also exhibited when we humbly bow before Christ in repentance and faith, for then we find forgiveness. Thank God for His grace, for without it we would have no hope!

Grace and truth come through Jesus Christ.
JOHN 1:17

DECEMBER 1

Young people seek adventure and excitement; but youth wants more—it wants something to believe in; it wants a cause to give itself to and a flag to follow. Without a purpose greater than themselves, young people know they will end up with empty hearts and meaningless lives. The only cause that is big enough to satisfy the yearning of our hearts is the cause of Jesus Christ; and its flag is the blood-stained body that was lifted on the Cross of Calvary for the redemption of the world.... We can each have a part, using the unique gifts and opportunities God has given us.... How are you responding to His call?

JANUARY 29

Recently some computers in our office were attacked by a major computer virus. Thinking they were opening a legitimate e-mail, the staff suddenly found their computers running amuck, unable to function as they were designed to do.... God created our first parents perfect and without sin...but then they rebelled against God, sin entered the world—and since that day, the human heart has been infected with the deadly "virus" of sin.... But Christ came to conquer the "virus" of sin! When He enters our lives, He begins to remake us from within. The "virus" no longer has absolute control. And some day God will remove the "virus" of sin forever, and all creation will be renewed.

DECEMBER 2

Worry about what might happen makes even the smallest trouble seem huge. Nervously anticipating troubles that may never happen can crush our spirit.

Instead of "borrowing trouble" by constantly worrying about the future, listen instead to Jesus' promise: "Peace I leave with you, My peace I give you; not as the world gives do I give to you. Let not your heart be troubled, neither let it be afraid (John 14:27).

Whatever is worrying you right now, give it to Jesus and trust Him to take care of it. Let His peace replace your worry.

JANUARY 28

Once I stood in London to watch Queen Elizabeth return from an overseas trip. I saw the parade of dignitaries, the marching bands, the crack troops, the waving flags. I saw all the splendor that accompanies the homecoming of a queen. However, that was nothing compared to the homecoming of a true believer. At that moment of death, the believer enters heaven itself, carried upward by the angels to the glorious welcome awaiting the redeemed (Luke 16:22).... The way to heaven may lie through the valley of the shadow of death, but the angels accompany us all the way—and beyond is heaven, our glorious home.

DECEMBER 3

We Christians are not to be conformed to this world in the way we think. The world by its advertisements, its conversation, and its philosophy is engaged in a gigantic brainwashing.... Time yourself the next time you read the Bible and pray. Compare it to the amount of time you spend watching television or surfing the Internet. Is God getting His share of your time and attention?

Is the world shaping your mind—or Christ?

Let this mind be in you which was also in Christ Jesus. PHILIPPIANS 2:5

JANUARY 27

Not far from our home in North Carolina is Mt. Mitchell, the highest point in the eastern United States. On its ridges are old trees that have been stunted and gnarled by the hostile climate and the sparse rocky soil. But local craftsmen have told me that if one of these trees finally dies, its wood is highly prized—and the reason is because it is so strong.... The roots are like an anchor helping them survive the storms, and they also draw up the soil's nutrients, helping them grow stronger. Make sure your soul is firmly planted in Christ, so you may be "rooted and built up in Him and established in the faith" (Colossians 2:7).

DECEMBER 4

Almost 2000 years ago Jesus Christ won the decisive battle against sin and Satan, through His death and resurrection. Satan did his best to defeat God's plans, but he could not win against God's overwhelming power.... For you who believe in Jesus Christ, the future is assured. Tomorrow belongs to you! You await the distant trumpet announcing the coming of Jesus Christ. In the meantime let nothing discourage you. Keep your eyes on Christ and live each day as if He were coming tomorrow. After all, He might!

Abide in Him, that when He appears, we may...not be ashamed before Him at His coming. 1 JOHN 2:28

JANUARY 26

Just as surely as God implants the life cell in the tiny seed that produces the mighty oak...as surely as He instills the heartbeat in the life of the tiny infant yet unborn...as surely as He puts motion into the planets, stars, and heavenly bodies—so He implants His divine life in the hearts of those who earnestly seek Him through Christ.... But has it happened to you? If not, you are not only unfit for the kingdom of God—you are cheating yourself out of the greatest, most revolutionary experience known to any human being. By a simple prayer of faith ask Christ into your life right now. He will come in, and you will be born again!

DECEMBER 5

Before the power of the atom was discovered, science had to devise a way to smash the atom. The secret of the atom's immeasurable and limitless power was in its being crushed.... Dr. Edward Judson, at the dedication of a church in New York City, said, "Suffering and success go together. If you are succeeding without suffering, it is because others before you have suffered; if you are suffering without succeeding, it is that others after you may succeed." Admittedly, it's hard to "count it all joy" when suffering comes. But when it does, ask God to sanctify it and use it to make you steadfast in your faith.

JANUARY 25

Every year people write me saying how much they dread Christmas.... Did those wise men who journeyed hundreds of miles across the desert to seek out the infant Jesus ever feel that way?... I doubt it. In fact, as their journey neared its end we read they had "exceedingly great joy" (Matthew 2:10). What made the difference? Their focus was totally on Jesus.... Don't let this Christmas season overwhelm you. Don't feel you have to do everything, or go into debt just to impress other people. Focus instead on Jesus. Take time every day to read the prophecies of His coming, and the wonderful story of His birth. Make this Christmas one of "exceedingly great joy"!

DECEMBER 6

John Knox prayed, and the results caused Queen Mary to say that she feared the prayers of John Knox more than she feared the armies of Scotland. John Wesley prayed, and revival came to England, sparing that nation the horrors of the French Revolution. Jonathan Edwards prayed, and revival spread throughout the American colonies. History has been changed time after time because of prayer. I tell you, history could be changed again if people went to their knees in believing prayer. Even when times are bleak and the world scorns God, He still works through the prayers of His people. Pray today for revival in your nation, and around the world.

The effective, fervent prayer of a righteous man avails much. JAMES 5:16

JANUARY 24

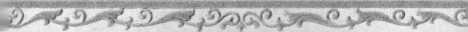

Some years ago a friend of mine was standing on top of a mountain in North Carolina. The roads in those days were filled with curves, and it was difficult to see very far ahead. This man saw two cars heading toward each other…. My friend shouted a warning, but the drivers couldn't hear, and there was a fatal crash. This is how God looks upon us in His omniscience…. Like the man on that mountain, He shouts His warnings at us—but we are too busy or too stubborn to listen. God sees the whole picture. He knows what is best for us, and He knows what will destroy us. Don't think your way is better than His, but listen to His Word—and obey.

DECEMBER 7

Because many do not believe in life after death, their writings are filled with tragedy and pessimism. The writings of William Faulkner, James Joyce, and many others are filled with pessimism, darkness, and tragedy. Sadly, the same was often true of their lives. How different from Jesus Christ who said, "I am the resurrection and the life. He who believes in Me shall never die" (John 11:25–26).... Because we know Christ is alive, we have hope—hope for the present and hope for life beyond the grave.

JANUARY 23

Parents who refuse to discipline their children are actually sending a signal, saying they don't care what happens to them…. The Bible…says to train our children in God's ways "precept upon precept, line upon line…here a little, there a little" (Isaiah 28:10). In other words, when a child is about to become a teenager, we can't suddenly say, "I've ignored it so far, but now I'll cram religion and morals into my child." It must start the very moment he or she has any understanding. But what we do is as important as what we say, for children usually acquire their parents' characteristics and habits. What are our children (and grandchildren) learning from us?

DECEMBER 8

The born-again Christian sees life not as a blurred, confused, meaningless mass, but as something planned and purposeful…. In Christ's first sermon at Nazareth, He said that one of the reasons He had come to earth was to preach "recovery of sight to the blind" (Luke 4:18)…. The Spirit of God helps us see our sin and our helplessness and shows us God's redeeming grace in Christ. The Spirit reveals the truth of Jesus' declaration: "I am the light of the world. He who follows Me shall not walk in darkness, but have the light of life" (John 8:12)…. In the midst of a world living in spiritual darkness, walk as a child of the light!…

JANUARY 22

One evening in Jerusalem I looked out my hotel window and saw the lights of Bethlehem in the distance. I thought about the response of the innkeeper when Mary and Joseph wanted to find a room where the Child could be born. The innkeeper was not hostile; he was not opposed to them but his inn was crowded, his hands were full, and his mind was preoccupied.... This is the answer that millions give today. It is the answer of preoccupation—not fierce opposition, not furious hatred, but unconcern about spiritual things. We are simply too preoccupied with other things to welcome Christ into our lives. Don't let that happen to you!

Behold, God is great, and we do not know Him. JOB 36:26

DECEMBER 9

The command to "be filled with the Spirit" actually has the idea of continuously being filled…. This verse might be translated, "Be filled and keep on being filled."

Dr. Merrill C. Tenney has compared this to the situation of an old-time farmhouse kitchen. In one corner was a sink; above it was a pipe through which came a continuous stream of water from the spring outside. The water, by running constantly, kept the sink brimful of good water. In the same way,… the Holy Spirit should flow within us constantly—and He will, as we yield ourselves to Christ's presence and power every day.

Be filled with the Spirit. EPHESIANS 5:18 NIV

JANUARY 21

When Paul approached the valley of the shadow of death he did not shudder with fear; rather he announced with a note of triumph, "The time of my departure is at hand (2 Timothy 4:6). The word departure in Paul's time literally meant to pull up anchor and set sail. Everything that happens prior to death is a preparation for the journey…. Separation always brings a tinge of sadness, but there is a high hope that we shall meet again. Such is the hope of every believing Christian as we stand at the grave…. We say "Goodbye," but only until that new day dawns and we are together with the Lord.

DECEMBER 10

Few people know how to rest these days. Even on vacation, many people rush to cram in as much as they can before returning to their jobs, where they spend twice as much energy catching up on the work and mail that has piled up in their absence.... Perhaps we have been looking for rest in the wrong places.... Jesus gives us the ultimate rest, the confidence we need, to escape the frustration and chaos of the world around us. Rest in Him and don't worry about what lies ahead. Jesus Christ has already taken care of tomorrow.

Come to Me, all you who labor and are heavy laden, and I will give you rest. MATTHEW 11:28

JANUARY 20

On that first Christmas night in Bethlehem, "God was manifested in the flesh" (1 Timothy 3:16). This manifestation was in the person of Jesus Christ. What an incredible truth! Think of it: The God of the universe came down from heaven that first Christmas night and took human form! As the words of the familiar Christmas carol declare, "Veiled in flesh the Godhead see; hail th' incarnate Deity." If you want to know what God is like, then take a long look at Jesus Christ—because He was God in human flesh. In Him were displayed not only the perfections that had been exhibited in the creation—such as wisdom, power, and majesty—but also such perfections as justice, mercy, grace, and love.

DECEMBER 11

What a joy it is to wake up in the morning and know He is with me, no matter what the day has in store. What a joy it is to look back in the evening and be able to thank Him for His faithfulness and to experience His peace. What a joy it is to know that some day soon the burdens of this life will be over and I will awaken to His presence.

JANUARY 19

Over two thousand years ago, on a night the world has come to call Christmas, a young Jewish maiden went through the experience countless mothers had before her: She brought forth a child. But this birth was like no other in the history of the human race.... As the angel had promised, "The Holy Spirit will come upon you, and the power of the Highest will overshadow you" (Luke 1:35).... This was the unique Son of God, sent from heaven to save us from our sins. Amid the glitter and busyness of the season, don't lose sight of the miracle of that first Christmas. With the wise men, let us fall down and worship Him (Matthew 2:11).

DECEMBER 12

"I am with you always, to the very end of the age" (Matthew 28:20 NIV). These words are Christ's promise to all His disciples, and it is a promise that is marvelously inclusive. No situation is excluded; no challenge is omitted. Dr. Handley Moule, the noted Greek scholar and Anglican Bishop of Durham (England) in another generation, maintained that the word always could be paraphrased to mean, "I am with you all the days, all day long." That means we can count on Christ's presence not only every day, but every moment of every day.

JANUARY 18

Imagine the scene in Bethlehem two thousand years ago. It was the night of nights, and yet it had begun as every other night had before it. But it was to become the greatest, most significant night in history. This was the night that would conquer darkness and bring in the day when there would be no more night. This was the night when those who sat in darkness would see a great light. This was the night God brought into the world the One who is "the light of the world." May His light shine in your life this Christmas season!

I am the light of the world. He who follows
Me shall not walk in darkness. John 8:12

DECEMBER 13

The Father's house will be a happy home because there will be work to do there. John wrote in Revelation 22:3, "His servants shall serve Him." Each one will be given exactly the task that suits his powers, his tastes, and his abilities. And the Father's house will be a happy home because friends will be there…. Not one of us who enters the Father's house will feel lonely or strange, for we who have put our trust in Christ are part of His family, sharing heaven's joys forever with all our brothers and sisters in Christ…. In the midst of earth's turmoil, keep your eyes on heaven!

JANUARY 17

Jesus came to the world so we could know, once and for all, that God is concerned about the way we live, the way we believe, and the way we die. God could have told us in other ways, of course—and He had, throughout the pages of the Old Testament.... But Jesus was the Living Word.... Every time He fed the hungry, He was saying, "I am the bread of life." Every time He healed a suffering person, He was saying, "It hurts Me to see you in pain." Every move He made, every miracle He performed, every word He spoke was for the purpose of reconciling a lost world to the loving, compassionate God.

DECEMBER 14

People deeply in love find absolute bliss simply being in each other's presence.

In the same way, simply being in the presence of God brings us great joy. It happens as we listen to Him speak in His word; it happens as we pray. But it also happens as we simply enjoy His presence—meditating on His goodness, delighting in the beauty of His creation, rejoicing in the life of a new baby or the surprise of an unexpected blessing…. Some day we will be in His presence forever; the Bible says, "God Himself will be with them" (Revelation 21:3)…. In the meantime, delight in His presence right now, for He is with you every hour of the day.

JANUARY 16

The title "Christ" means "anointed one." It is the term, in the Greek language, for the ancient Hebrew word "Messiah"—the anointed one whom God would send to save His people. Peter and his fellow Jews, the first believers of the early Christian Church, recognized Jesus Christ as the Messiah promised in the Old Testament. Their world was one of discouragement and despair, but the promised Messiah shone as a beacon in the darkness, and His light has never dimmed. "In Him was life, and the life was the light of men" (John 1:4). No matter how dark the world gets...no matter how dark our paths may seem... Jesus is still our life and light.

DECEMBER 15

How often have you found what you were looking for in life, only to realize it didn't bring you the satisfaction you thought it would? It is life's ultimate frustration—thinking we will find fulfillment in the things of this world. But they can never bring lasting happiness. As one bumper sticker I saw expressed it, "All I want is a little more than I have now."... Try putting Christ first and watch how your life is turned around. You will discover that He alone is the source of the love, peace, and joy you have been searching for.

JANUARY 15

Can you even begin to imagine the Father's emotions that first Christmas as His dearly loved Son left heaven for earth, knowing He would one day go to the Cross, "despised and rejected by men, a Man of sorrows and acquainted with grief" (Isaiah 53:3)? We rightly focus on God's love for us. But don't lose sight of what it cost the Father to send His beloved Son into the world. Why did He do it? Because "God so loved the world that He gave His only begotten Son, that whoever believes in Him should not perish but have everlasting life" (John 3:16). God loves the Son—and He loves you as well.

DECEMBER 16

Conflict, discontent, and unhappiness plague people everywhere. But suppose a cure could be found for humanity's ills. It would cause a worldwide stampede! The most thrilling news in the world is that there is a cure! God has provided the medicine—and that "medicine" is Christ. Through Him our sins can be forgiven, and by His Holy Spirit within us our lives can be changed and renewed…. Our souls can know peace, a peace that is not dependent on outward circumstances. This cure was provided two thousand years ago by Jesus Christ's death and resurrection for us. Is He working daily in your life, changing you and making you more like Him?

JANUARY 14

Only two groups of people gathered at God's invitation to pay Him homage when He was born. One was the shepherds—lowly, at the bottom of the social ladder, uneducated, unsophisticated. The other was the wise men—intellectuals, from another race and country, wealthy, respected. The two groups could hardly have been more different!

God brought both groups to Bethlehem—one by an angelic announcement, one by the appearance of a miraculous star. And by bringing both, God was telling us that Jesus is the Savior for everyone.... No matter who you are in the eyes of others, you need Christ. And no matter what you have done, He loves you and stands ready to welcome you.

DECEMBER 17

In the midst of the Lord's Prayer are these familiar words: "Give us this day our daily bread" (Matthew 6:11). They remind us that we are dependent on God for everything, and He is the giver of every blessing. "Every good gift and every perfect gift is from above, and comes down from the Father of lights" (James 1:17).... This prayer reminds us also of Jesus' words: "I am the bread of life. He who comes to Me shall never hunger" (John 6:35). Thank God for all His gifts—especially Christ, the greatest gift of all.

JANUARY 13

During the First World War, on Christmas Eve, the battlefield was strangely quiet.... Softly one lad began to hum "Silent Night." Others took up the chorus until the trenches resounded with the Christmas song. When they finished they were astonished to hear the song echoing from the trenches across no-man's-land: In their own tongue the other soldiers also sang "Silent Night."... How different this world would be if we could unite together around that "Holy Infant so tender and mild."... Full peace will come only when Christ returns. But until that day we can know His peace in our hearts can be messengers of His peace in the world, as we commit our lives to Him.

DECEMBER 18

In His Steps, by Charles M. Sheldon, tells of a challenge given by a pastor to his people to pledge for one year not to do anything without first asking the question: "What would Jesus do?"... If someone posed the same question to us, what would be our response? Do we live our lives with the thought, "What would Jesus do?" Do we put it into practice every day?

We are in Him who is true, in His Son Jesus Christ. 1 John 5:20

JANUARY 12

The Babe in the manger of Bethlehem grew up to become our crucified and risen Savior—and the world has never been the same. His compassion has made the world more compassionate. His healing touch has made the world more self-effacing. Christ drew a rainbow of hope around the shoulders of men and women and gave them something to live for…. Christ came into the world and made it a better place. And He will do the same for you, if you will open your life to Him.

DECEMBER 19

Tom Allan, Scotland's famous preacher, was brought to Christ while a soldier was singing, "Were you there when they crucified my Lord?" He said it was neither the song nor the voice, but the spirit in which the soldier sang…. Jesus said, "You are the light of the world…. Let your light so shine before [others], that they may see your good works, and glorify your Father in heaven" (Matthew 5:14, 16). Our faith becomes stronger as we express it; a growing faith is a sharing faith. Pray now for those you know who need Christ, and ask God to help you be a witness to them—by the life you live and the words you speak.

JANUARY 11

Something about Jesus inspired allegiance, loyalty, and homage. Wise men brought Him gifts. Shepherds fell down and worshiped Him. Herod, realizing that there is never room for two thrones in one kingdom, sought His life. As Jesus began His ministry, His claims upon people's lives were total and absolute. He allowed no divided loyalty. He demanded and received complete adoration and devotion.... His words caused even His most avowed enemies to say, "No man ever spoke like this Man!" (John 7:46).... We cannot understand Christ until we understand that He was the King of kings and the Lord of lords. Like Thomas, our only response must be to bow down and confess, "My Lord and my God!" (John 20:28).

DECEMBER 20

Jesus told His disciples: "Seek first the kingdom of God and His righteousness, and all these things shall be added to you" (Matthew 6:33). The "things" He spoke of were the basic needs of life: food, drink, clothes, shelter. He told us not to make these things the chief goal of our lives, but to "seek...the kingdom." There, if we will take it, is the secret of happiness: "Seek first the kingdom of God...." How do we do this? By submitting ourselves without reserve to Jesus Christ as King of our lives every day. This is the path of true happiness.

JANUARY 10

I never come to Christmas without thinking of the thousands of people who are lonely and troubled at this time of year. I have had psychiatrists tell me their schedules are overloaded with people who find the Christmas season almost more than they can bear because of their loneliness and isolation. Christmas is God's reminder that we are not alone. God revealed in this life, death, and resurrection of Jesus a reconciling love that rescues us from separation and loneliness. We are not alone; God has come down from heaven to tell us He loves us! At this Christmas season you can be assured that Jesus Christ is here.

DECEMBER 21

The blood of Christ may seem to be a grim, repulsive subject to those who do not realize its true significance; but to those who have been rescued from sin's chains, Christ's nail-pierced hands are beautiful beyond measure, for they tell us of His love and His willingness to save us regardless of the cost.

In Him we have redemption through His blood. EPHESIANS 1:7

JANUARY 9

Christmas is the celebration of the event that set heaven to singing, an event that gave the stars of the night sky a new brilliance. Christmas tells us that at a specific time and at a specific place a specific Person was born…. From the lips of Him who came fell these words: "The Son of Man has come to seek and to save that which was lost" (Luke 19:10). Like piercing trumpets, these words heralded the breaking in of the Divine to human history. They declare that heaven has come to our rescue and that God has not left us to stumble alone on Earth's pathway. What a wonderful and glorious hope we have because of that first Christmas!

DECEMBER 22

When Charles Wesley experienced the joy of divine forgiveness, he told a Moravian friend of his new sense of pardon, and added, "I suppose I had better keep silent about it."

"Oh, no, my brother," came the reply. "If you had a thousand tongues, you should go and use them all for Jesus." Charles Wesley went home and wrote the great hymn:
"Oh for a thousand tongues to sing
My great Redeemer's praise,
The glories of my God and King,
The triumphs of His grace!"

…Have you received God's gift of forgiveness? If you have, thank Him for it—and if not, by faith invite Christ into your life today.

JANUARY 8

Christ came into a world that had problems much like the ones we grapple with today.... To those without the joy of living, Jesus said, "I have come that they may have life, and that they may have it more abundantly" (John 10:10). To those who bore the chafing burden of the guilt of sin, He said, "Be of good cheer; your sins are forgiven you" (Matthew 9:2). To the friendless He said, "No longer do I call you servants...but I have called you friends" (John 15:15).... Christ still comes to us to cleanse our guilt, give us hope for the future, and heal our hurts with His love.

DECEMBER 23

Some years ago I visited a man who was wealthy and successful, the envy of all his friends and business associates. But as we talked, he broke down in tears, confessing that he was miserable inside. Wealth had not been able to fill the empty place in his heart. A few hours later I visited another man who lived only a few miles away. His cottage was humble, and he had almost nothing...yet his face was radiant as he told me about the work he was doing for Christ and how Christ had filled his life with meaning and purpose. I went away convinced that the second man was really a rich man.... A spirit of thankfulness makes all the difference.

JANUARY 7

The centuries have rolled by, and still the world longs for and looks for the peace the angels sang about on that first Christmas morning. Even the land of His birth often seems torn by violence and conflict.... I know of no country that is completely safe or completely at peace. The greatest war of all, however is the war between us and God, as we stubbornly rebel against His authority and defiantly seize control of our lives apart from Him. But now the war can be over, as we yield ourselves to Christ as our Lord. Then we have peace—peace with God, peace in our hearts, and peace with each other. Is the war over in your life?

DECEMBER 24

There was once a little boy who was riding alone in a train, and the scenery was not too interesting. A woman sitting beside him asked, "Are you tired of the long ride?"

The boy smiled and said, "I'm a little tired, but I don't mind it much. You see, my father is going to meet me when I get there." Sometimes we get tired of the burdens of life, but we know that Jesus Christ will meet us at the end of our own life's journey—and that makes all the difference…. Knowing we will be with Christ forever far outweighs our burdens today! Keep your eyes on eternity!

JANUARY 6

"She brought forth her firstborn Son,...and laid Him in a manger, because there was no room for them in the inn" (Luke 2:7).... There was no room for Jesus in the world that He had made—imagine! Things have not really changed since that Bethlehem night over two thousand years ago.... We fit Him in when it is convenient for us, but we become irritated when He makes demands on us. If God would only stay in his little box and come out when we pull the string! Our lives are so full. There is so much to be done. But in all our busy activities are we in danger of excluding from our hearts and lives the One who made us?

DECEMBER 25

After His resurrection Jesus came to His disciples, meeting them between the garden with its empty tomb and the city with its mob still passionate with hate. He said to them, "Do not be afraid. Go and tell my brethren" (Matthew 28:10). In the midst of a world filled with danger, hatred, and war, the words of our Lord Jesus Christ are just as relevant as when He spoke them. He still says to all who love Him, "Do not be afraid."

Who shall separate us from the love of Christ? ROMANS 8:35

JANUARY 5

[Jesus]...came on a mission of love and mercy, sent by the Father. An angel announced His conception and gave Him His name. The heavenly host sang a glorious anthem at His birth. By the extraordinary star, the very heavens indicated His coming... Yet no sooner did He enter our world than Herod decreed His death and labored to accomplish it.... He assumed our human nature with all its infirmities, and weakness, and capacity for suffering. He came as a child of the poorest parents. His entire life was one long pathway of humiliation. Now He is in heaven, no longer limited by time and space. And some day He will come again—this time in glory—to take us to Himself.

DECEMBER 26

When David Livingstone returned to his native Scotland after sixteen difficult years as a missionary and explorer in Africa, his body was emaciated by...fevers that had coursed through his veins during the years.... His left arm hung useless at his side, the result of being mangled by a lion. Speaking to the students at Glasgow University, he said, "Shall I tell you what sustained me during the hardship and loneliness of my exile? It was Christ's promise, 'Lo, I am with you always, even to the end of the age'" (Matthew 28:20).... No matter what trials we face, Christ never leaves us.... Keep that promise before you today—and always.

JANUARY 4

The end of another year is approaching, and people are already predicting what the new year holds…. The fact is, no one knows the future—except God…. He knows it all—because He created it in the first place. We will always be bewildered and confused by what we don't know, if we are honest. We don't even know our immediate futures; as James said, "You do not know what will happen tomorrow" (James 4:14). What should this mean? It should give us humility before God, and it should give us trust—trust in the God who does know our futures, and who works all things for His glory. You can trust all your tomorrows to Him!

DECEMBER 27

Near my home is a spring that never varies its flow. Floods may rage, but its output doesn't increase. A long summer's drought may come, but it won't decrease. Its flow is steady, reliable, and unending. Such is the peace we all yearn for—and such is the peace Jesus promises to all who trust in Him: "The water that I shall give him will become in him a fountain of water springing up into everlasting life…. My peace I give to you" (John 4:14; 14:27). Have you come to that unending spring—which is Christ? Are you coming to Him each day?

JANUARY 3

Alexander Nowell once said, "God does not comfort us that we may be comforted but that we may be comforters." We are to pass along the comfort with which God has comforted us. Look around you. There are countless opportunities to comfort others, not only in the loss of a loved one, but also in the daily distress that so often creeps into our lives. One of Paul's companions on some of his missionary journeys was named Joseph, but "the apostles called [him] Barnabas which means Son of Encouragement)" (Acts 4:36 NIV). Will you be a Barnabas to someone today?

Blessed be the God...of all comfort.
2 CORINTHIANS 1:3

DECEMBER 28

When hard times come we easily get discouraged. But behind the clouds God is still present, and can even use them to water our souls with unexpected blessings. Longfellow once wrote: "Be still, sad heart, and cease repining; behind the clouds is the sun still shining." As God's people wandered in the wilderness, He declared, "Behold, I come to you in a thick cloud" (Exodus 19:9). Each of us experiences clouds in life—sometimes slight but sometimes dark and frightening. Whatever clouds you face today, ask Jesus, the light of the world, to help you look behind the cloud to see His glory and His plans for you.

JANUARY 2

We must guard against appetites that blight the conscience, wither the soul, and weaken our witness for Christ. Perhaps many things are lawful, but are they expedient? Are they a harmful example to others? As long as we are in this world, our old nature will try to defeat us and turn us away from Christ. But learn to recognize the warning signs, and commit your mind and body to Christ "as instruments of righteousness."

Present...your members as instruments of righteousness to God. ROMANS 6:13

DECEMBER 29

Out West an old sheepherder had a violin, but it was out of tune. He had no way of tuning it, so in desperation he wrote to one of the radio stations and asked them at a certain hour on a certain day to strike the tone "A." The officials of the station decided they would accommodate the old fellow, and on that particular day the true tone of "A" was broadcast. His fiddle was thus tuned, and once more his cabin echoed with joyful music…. As this new year begins, ask God to help you tune your life every day to His Word, so you can bring harmony and joy to those around you.

JANUARY 1

If you are a parent you've undoubtedly had the experience of having your children complain after Christmas is over, disappointed they didn't get the gift they wanted or bored with the ones they received…. God our Father has given gifts to each of us, and I pray we may never become discontent or bored with them…. None of us has every gift, but every Christian has at least one, to be used for one purpose: to build up Christ's body, the Church (Ephesians 4:11-12). What spiritual gift has God given you? Don't worry about those you don't have. Be content with those God has given you, and use them for His glory.

DECEMBER 30

Many years ago I was visiting the dining room of the United States Senate. As I was speaking to various people, one of the senators said, "Billy, we're having a discussion about pessimism and optimism. Are you a pessimist or an optimist?" I smiled and said, "I'm an optimist." He asked "Why?" I replied, "I've read the last page of the Bible."…

As another year ends, no doubt you have had your share of joys and disappointments. Don't live in the past, but "be patient and stand firm, because the Lord's coming is near" (James 5:8 NIV).

DECEMBER 31

Presented To

....

From

....

Date

....